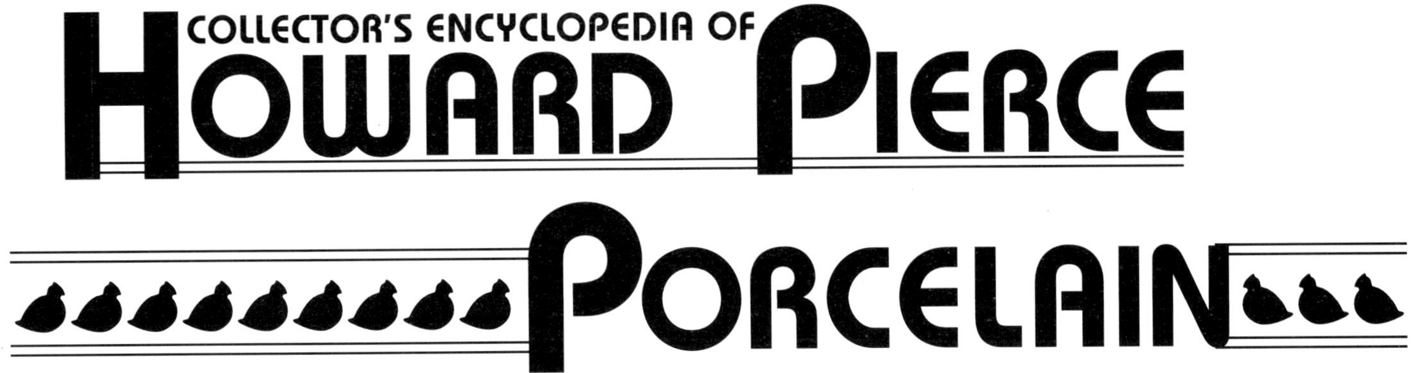

Collector's Encyclopedia of Howard Pierce Porcelain

Identification and Values

Darlene Hurst Dommel

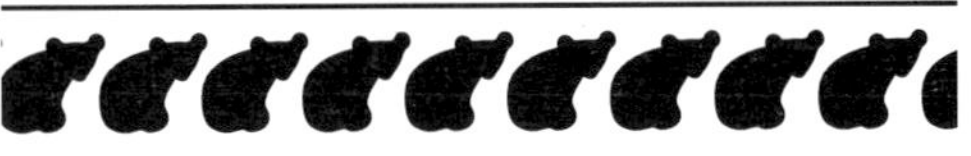

COLLECTOR BOOKS

A Division of Schroeder Publishing Co., Inc.

The current values in this book should be used only as a guide. They are not intended to set prices, which vary from one section of the country to another. Auction prices as well as dealer prices vary greatly and are affected by condition as well as demand. Neither the Author nor the Publisher assumes responsibility for any losses that might be incurred as a result of consulting this guide.

Searching For A Publisher?

We are always looking for knowledgeable people considered to be experts within their fields. If you feel that there is a real need for a book on your collectible subject and have a large comprehensive collection, contact Collector Books.

On this cover: Mountain sheep ram, $80.00 – 100.00; "Family Group," $175.00 – 225.00; covey of three quail $50.00 – 65.00; mother and bear cub, $50.00 – 75.00.

Cover design by Beth Summers
Book design by Mary Ann Dorris

Additional copies of this book may be ordered from:

COLLECTOR BOOKS
P.O. Box 3009
Paducah, Kentucky 42002-3009

@$24.95. Add $2.00 for postage and handling.

CONTENTS

ACKNOWLEDGMENTS

This book is dedicated to the late Howard Pierce and his family — Ellen Pierce, Linda Pierce Picciotto, Janet Pierce Self, and Jerry and Barbara Pierce. Their generous time, information, and collections made this book possible. All archival photographs in this book are courtesy of the Pierce family.

The special efforts of Ron and Juvelyn Nickel and Bob and Clara Sweet are greatly appreciated as they added new dimensions to the book through their photographs, information, and pricing assistance.

I want to thank my husband Jim who recognized the book's potential and provided support, encouragement, and assistance throughout. Thanks to my children Diann, Christine, and David for their support, and especially Diann for her advice and computer expertise.

I am also grateful to my editor, Lisa Stroup, and my photographers — Peter Lee, Peter Atherton, Vince Klassen, Jim Dommel, Juvelyn Nickel, and Bob Sweet.

PREFACE

Prices, based on mint condition, are only a guide providing a general overview of scarcity and quality. Rarity is sometimes difficult to determine, but some items considered rare are so marked. One-of-a-kind or extremely rare pieces are not priced since they seldom appear on the market.

All porcelain pieces are some variation of satin-matte brown/white glaze, unless specified otherwise.

Because of the number of shapes produced, it was not possible to include all shapes and variations, only to indicate the range available. Occasionally, shapes are repeated to show other glazes and colors.

Howard Pierce and his concrete sculpture, "Big Horn Henry."

INTRODUCTION

California art pottery has been discovered. Recent books and articles extol its virtues as collector interest increases and prices elevate.

Working in Claremont and Joshua Tree, Howard Pierce exemplified the California artist mystique. In a land of immigrants, California artists were "subject to influence, open to search and ready to do it themselves."[1] Pierce displayed the originality of style, designs, and glazes characteristic of California pottery. A remarkable artisan, Howard Piece produced a wide range of creations in porcelain and other media, scanning a 50 year career.

After World War II, Japan with its widely available clay, low wages, and time-honored technology streamlined its ceramic industry and vastly accelerated production. Without tariffs or import quotas, the United States became a ready market.

Inexpensive Japanese ceramics drove many of America's own potteries out of business. California potteries were part of this trend, with the demise of most. "By 1948, the peak years for the industry, over eight hundred ceramic concerns were in operation throughout California. The number of producers had been reduced to a fraction of the post-war high by the early sixties."[2]

Howard Pierce's small home-based business was a phenomenal exception. He met the tremendous competition from home and abroad, continuing to produce quality ware.

Why did Howard Pierce's efforts thrive while many others failed? Scrutiny of Pierce's assessment and adaptation to market needs, selection and direct study of subjects, love of work, personal focus, quality emphasis, and development of style may hold the answers.

A realistic man, Howard Pierce "harnessed his talent into a product orientation."[3] He assessed public desires, adapting to the market, changing designs to meet public demand. Pierce produced for the masses, at reasonable prices, for daily use in their homes.

Howard Pierce chose his artistic subjects mainly from nature. As Henry David Thoreau stated, "We need the tonic of wildness — we can never have enough of nature."[4] By focusing on animals and birds, Pierce turned to perennially popular subjects. "The most ancient works of art which we possess are representations of animals, often strikingly characteristic, carved in stag's horn or bone and found in caves."[5] Throughout the centuries, figures of animals and birds, familiar or fictitious, have been increasingly in demand.

Howard Pierce lived among the creatures he portrayed, observing them in their natural habitats, studying their actions and movements. The nature of animals and birds "cannot really be understood from drawings in a book or a single photograph."[6] "The more the artist studies nature the nearer he approaches to the true and perfect idea of art."[7]

Pottery production became the dominating focus of Howard Pierce's life. His long hours and emphasis on efficient methods made him a prolific potter. "If that's what you go after, then you can't go after fifty other things. You have to work very hard at it. It has to be an obsession...the motivating factor of your existence."[8]

"Love of what he was doing, with all its rewards, was what counted."[9] Howard Pierce loved his work and way of life. California with its "benevolent climate and room to grow" provided "a world apart — a world which could be remade in one's own vision — in which one's desired life could be realized and one's influence felt."[10]

While many United States potteries attempted to compete with Japanese imports by making cheaper products, Howard Pierce never lowered standards or compromised quality.

"The contemporary look in porcelain"[11] reads the Pierce advertising slogan. Pierce creations, with their sleek, stylized lines, looked contemporary or modern. These images were groundbreaking in their day. Porcelain was the chosen pottery type. Pierce possessed the craftsmanship skills required for its production and preferred the durable results.

Using his innate artistic ability and inspired by others, Howard Pierce's own distinctive style evolved. Interpretation was key. In an earlier century, an 1887 book advised, "the artist must create or interpret, not just copy nature."[12] Ernest Batchelder, already a successful California potter in the early 1900s, felt that "copying nature directly would not suffice because design becomes increasingly uninteresting the closer it approaches exact replication."[13]

Capturing the essence of his subjects was perhaps Howard Pierce's greatest artistic gift. By picturing the "essential character of a species, drawing attention to distinctive features,"[14] Pierce made his creations "look alive."[15] John Ruskin described essence as "the mysterious sense of unaccountable life in things themselves."[16] "The intangible qualities which bring a piece to life are never fully understood,"[17] according to master potter Warren McKenzie. However, "Our instincts react whether or not our intellects understand it."[18]

HISTORY

Born and raised in Chicago, Howard Webster Pierce showed an early interest in art, although his father was an electrical engineer and his family was not arts oriented. Painting lessons at age 13 revealed that was not his forte. Howard's early talents were sketching and, especially, sculpting. He received a high school award for a plaster copy of an Abraham Lincoln statue when he was 17.

After high school, Pierce went to the University of Illinois for a year. The following year, he attended The Art Institute of Chicago while helping care for his dying father.

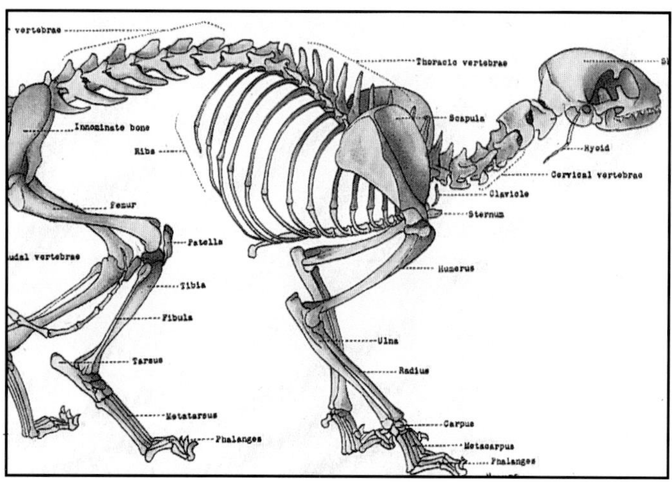

Pierce anatomical drawing of a cat.

Pursuing a childhood dream to be a medical illustrator, Howard also took some pre-med courses. Upon successfully sculpting some models for an American Medical Association exhibit for a physician, Pierce received a payment which changed his life — a Harley-Davidson.

At age 20, in the middle of the Depression, Howard Pierce's greatest adventure began. "After the death of his father and with little money to his name, he started around the world on that motorcycle. On that voyage, and for the rest of his life, Howard knew that he need not be a 'starving artist.' Art is needed at all times, he found, as he paid his way around making on-the-spot pencil sketches of people all over the world."[1]

In 1934, upon returning from the Far East, Howard went to Pasadena, California, to live with his aunt. He attended Pomona College for a year. His formal art training was limited to three years, but Howard's best education came from "learning by doing."[2]

Howard Pierce, Pasadena, California, 1935.

William Manker, an exceptional potter-instructor, became a mentor for Howard Pierce. Manker had served an apprenticeship with Ernest A. Batchelder, an influential Arts and Crafts movement proponent. Starting with his own one-man studio pottery, William Manker Ceramics soon prospered and expanded to larger facilities in Claremont, California. Manker designed and modeled his own modern shapes, with outstanding glazes his greatest achievement.

In 1938, Howard Pierce modeled a miniature fawn figurine which he sold to Manker. Manker needed a worker for two to three days at 45 cents an hour. Howard stayed on for three years, becoming production manager. Manker, also a ceramics instructor at Scripps College and the Claremont Graduate School, taught Howard the business.

Howard at Manker Ceramics.

As a freelancer, Howard did some work for hire on contract with other California potteries. Howard made his first molds for Kay Finch Ceramics, a successful 30s and 40s California pottery. Kay Finch met Howard when she studied with William Manker. According to family members, Howard also made several molds for other companies at various times.

Howard established his own studio at La Verne in 1941. William Manker was not interested in figurines and Howard "liked making figurines better than bowls."[3] He started making pewter figurines "so not to create direct competition for his former employer."[4]

Metalcraft was Howard's first entrepreneur project. By 1941, eighteen lapel pin designs were available in solid pewter or copper finish. Motifs included lamb, giraffe, colt, greyhound, cat, fish, camel, ostrich, gazelle, swan, elephant, horse head, Scottish terrier, pigeon, horse, eagle, and crane. A 1941 advertisement of two fawn variations denotes, "This pewter beastie manages to combine shyness with a certain insolent charm."[5] He also produced small metal figures.

During World War II doing defense work in drafting at Douglas Long Beach, Howard made the pins on weekends in a shed behind his Anaheim house. According to his wife, Ellen, the pins were sold to fellow workers at his plant and sometimes brought in more money than his Douglas salary.

Some pins were also available in copper-finish. The small figures were made of lead. All pewter items were highly polished before sale and were tarnish proof.

Howard devised an innovative method to paint some of the figures. They were fastened with clothes pins onto a wagon wheel. As the wheel went around, each pin was dipped into the color and was dry by the time it reached the wagon wheel top.

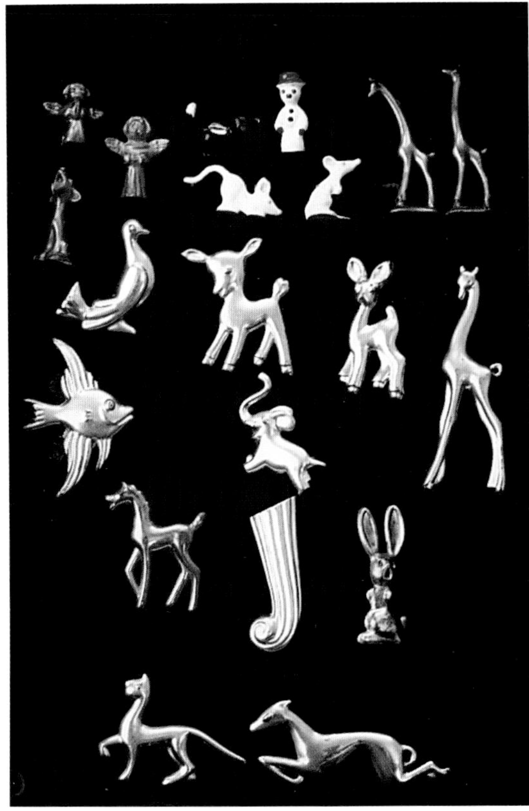

Pewter, copper-finish, and painted pins and figurines, sizes range from 2" to 5½" high, figurines are unmarked, pins are marked "HOWARD PIERCE," $125.00 – 150.00+ each. Painted figurines in photograph include two mice, snowman, and a skunk. A horse pin and two giraffes, two angels and a dog were made with copper finish. An elephant, giraffe, rabbit, cat, dog, dove, fish, swirled design, and two deer are pewter pins. (Pierce Family Collection)

Metalcraft mark.

PEWTER OR COPPER PINS

for Fall Costume Jewelry

$1 Retailers

Designed and produced in Southern California by Howard Pierce, there are about 18 smart animal designs available, each fitted with a good quality safety-type pin.

$6 a dozen

Assorted designs in either solid pewter or copper finish.

FRANK ROGERS

712 S. Olive St. **Los Angeles**

Reprinted from THE GIFT AND ART BUYER, *October,* 1941

Advertisement of pewter and copper pins.

Pewter advertisement.

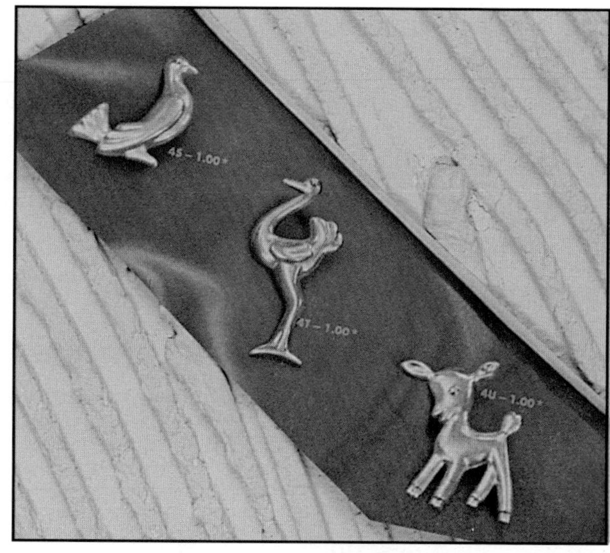

Pewter and copper pins, $125.00 – 150.00+ each.

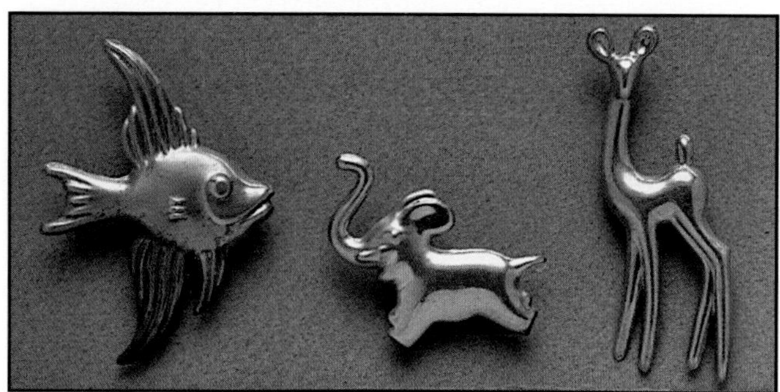

Pewter pins, $125.00 – 150.00+ each.

Ellen Van Voorhis met Howard Pierce, a patient of her dentist father, in 1940. His striking red Chevy convertible attracted her attention. A junior high National City art teacher, Ellen had previously lived with her family in Elgin, Illinois, where she graduated from the Chicago Art Institute.

After their 1941 marriage, the Pierces both quit their jobs. Having taught art for 10 years, Ellen "had it with teaching,"[6] and was ready to begin working with Howard. They became a very effective professional team. It would be impossible to accurately discuss Howard Pierce porcelains without including Ellen, a talented artisan herself.

Howard and Ellen in studio.

Ellen and Howard trimming and sponging, July 1984.

Howard credited his sustained success to Ellen's "concern for his audience."[7] Realizing that Ellen had a "good idea of what would sell,"[8] Howard listened carefully to her suggestions and made appropriate changes when necessary.

Ellen's constructive criticism also helped Howard "keep the delicate balance between commerce and art. She's my severest critic."[9] When Howard's artware became too realistic and lost its artistic appeal, Ellen told him, "It doesn't look like you."[10] Even if she felt the piece would sell well, Ellen wouldn't allow him to sacrifice his artistic integrity.

The special bond, which frequently develops in married couples who have worked together all their lives, was very evident in the Pierce relationship. Besides their love for art, the Pierces shared a passion for California — its land, flora, and fauna. For example, Ellen described her sorrow in seeing her first pair of bighorned sheep at their home after Howard died. "Howard would have loved to see them — a mother and father on their mountain."[11]

Ellen kept two artistic endeavors for herself — weaving and sewing. Ellen excelled as a weaver and continues with this craft.

Ellen thrived on her partnership role within the relationship and their shared goals. Howard was obviously appreciative of Ellen's influence on his work. Talking about his ware, Howard frequently included Ellen. "We're known for our ceramics all over the country."[12] Within their desert community, a local newspaper noted after Howard's death, "the beautiful sculptures they gave to us will serve as a memorial of this lovely couple. They made a difference."

Howard and Ellen's three children, twins Janet and Linda born in 1942 and Jerry in 1952, all grew up in the pottery business. Because the studio was attached to the house, they were actively interested in Howard's work. Ellen related that when they got home from school, they would dash through the house, calling a greeting to her, as they made a beeline for the studio.

Howard at left, Jerry, Janet, Linda in back, and Ellen at right.

Since Howard enjoyed having the children in the studio, "he'd put up with anything."[13] As young children, they liked mixing clay and forming their own pieces. Howard made things especially for them, like a plaster tunnel system for their white rat.

As they grew older, all three started to help make the pottery. "It was a fun thing, not work we were expected to do."[14] During his high school years and summer, Jerry worked with his father on a regular basis.

Boy Scout Court of Honor, 1966. Howard was a leader when Jerry became an Eagle Scout.

Opening the kiln.

Other workers, besides family members, were used during heavy production periods. Carl Lawrence, not a relative, but affectionately referred to as "Uncle Carl," worked for the Pierces for years. Occasionally, other people also helped. However, all did the same tasks as Ellen and the children — casting, sponging, and trimming only. Howard exclusively did all other aspects of the process.

For the family, "Opening the kiln was like Christmas. We would rush in to see the beautiful things. The things we had made would sometimes explode and wreck other things."[15] The kiln was fired every other day and opened as an eagerly awaited family ritual. As Ellen said, "I never tired of it — to see what had happened."[16]

Working alone in an isolated shop, not as part of an active network of other artists for exchange of ideas, Howard relied on his family members. They served the important roles of colleagues and critics. At the breakfast table, Howard would ask Ellen and his children for their opinions of his creations. "Some things we rejected — if no one liked something, he threw it out."[17] Sometimes Howard listened to his aunt. "If she liked a piece, he could be reasonably certain that it wouldn't sell well!"[18]

Names were a Pierce family tradition. When the girls were very young, they called Howard " Fa Fa" which later became "Fadee." Ellen was "Mother" to her own children, but "Marner" to some of the grandchildren. Animals and cars were sometimes named. When unique Pierce figurines were made in very limited quantities, they were often named, for example, "Beverly the Hippo." One monkey set was named "Pete and Repeat."

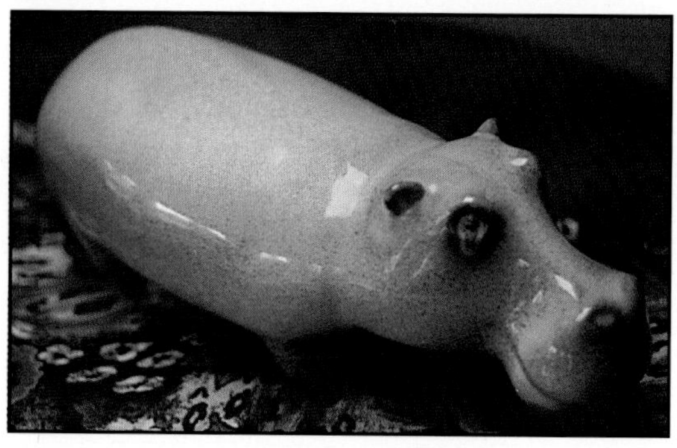

Extremely rare "Beverly the Hippo," 9" x 20". This was the largest porcelain that Howard fired. (Pierce Family Collection)

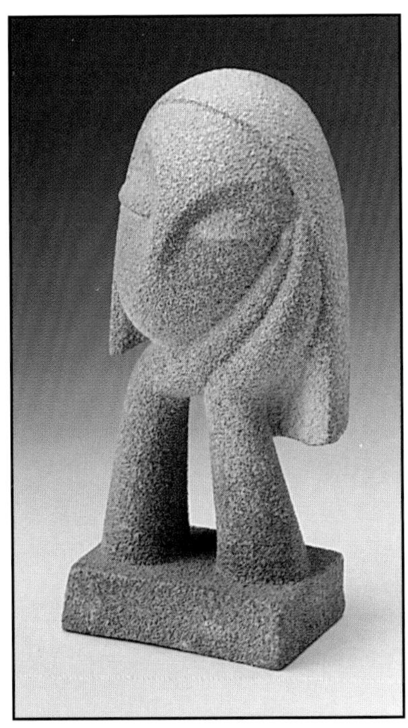

Extremely rare "Sandra" porcelain sculpture, $11^{1}/_{2}$" x $5^{1}/_{2}$, incised by hand "HOWARD PIERCE." (Pierce Family Collection)

"Ferdinand the Bull" in high gloss blue glaze with striking blue highlights, $3^{1}/_{4}$" x $5^{1}/_{2}$", "HOWARD PIERCE" brown ink stamp and hand signed "Pierce" in black ink, $75.00 – 85.00.

Each year in December, Howard and the family would decorate the front of the house with home-made decorations: plaster icicles, a sleigh and wire reindeer on the roof, a Santa scene among the succulents, etc. Their house was repeatedly on the list of "sights to see" in Claremont at Christmas time.

In his own way, Howard participated in his children's activities. For example, teachers were invited to the studio to cast their own mugs. At birthday parties, Pierce creations were a special treat as each guest was allowed to choose one. When the girls graduated from Claremont High School in 1960, each graduate in the class received a Howard Pierce-designed replica of the school mascot, the wolf.

"Ferdinand the Bull," brown and white, $3^{1}/_{4}$" x $5^{1}/_{2}$", black ink stamp "HOWARD PIERCE," $75.00 – 85.00; whitish, 6" x 9", black ink stamp "HOWARD PIERCE" and signed in black ink "Howard Pierce 84," $100.00 – 120.00. (Pierce Family Collection)

"Wolf," the school mascot, 4" x $2^{1}/_{2}$", "CSHS" impressed into one side and "1960" into the other, $175.00 – 200.00. (Ron and Juvelyn Nickel Collection)

In the summer of 1984, their daughter, Linda, came home to learn the business. She was considering taking over when Howard retired. Howard felt that she had talent and Linda was trained in all phases of the process. She enjoyed the creativity of making things. However, the pottery business did not suit her lifestyle. As a wife, mother, and elementary school teacher, she didn't want to work "ten hours a day, as a total commitment, like Fadee."[19]

Master and pupil, July 1984, pouring a mold. The head of an eagle sculpture can be seen on the table.

During this period, Linda designed a wood duck, the only Howard Pierce porcelains product ever designed by anyone other than Howard. Linda's duck was produced and sold for awhile. Later, Howard designed his own duck, which was similar.

Linda's duck, 3¾" x 5½", black ink stamp "HOWARD PIERCE," $75.00 – 85.00. (Pierce Family Collection)

Howard always kept his eye on the bottom line, with his pottery productions "based on money."[20] He needed to make a living for his family.

A self-sufficient man, Howard built their Claremont house out of cement blocks. A shed made from roofing materials was home for the Pierces and their three-year-old twin daughters until the house was completed. Howard did all he could himself — masonry, carpentry, electrical, and plumbing work. Ellen recalled with pleasure receiving a cement mixer as her birthday gift during this time.

Howard in front of studio/home he built in Claremont.

Although they lived frugally, Ellen stated, "We had anything we wanted. We saved our money and never bought on credit, even new cars."[21] They also put their three children through college to become a teacher, registered nurse, and an electrical engineer.

Howard had learned some commercial aspects through his work with Manker. However, there was "no school to learn the commercial end."[22] Therefore, he learned from experience, as he called it "fooling around and experimenting."[23]

Above all, Howard Pierce was a commercial artist. Howard tried to determine what the public wanted and then create for that demand. For example, he said, " I love abstraction but settle for the semi-abstract,"[24] as the truly abstract would not sell. Even in semi-retirement he continued to make what he knew would sell. Howard tells of really liking a huge horse sculpture. But, when no one else liked it, not even Ellen, he "threw it over the cliff."[25]

Howard Pierce porcelains always sold for reasonable prices. Ellen related that keeping prices low was paramount so that the public could afford to own his pieces. He also found it difficult to discuss prices with customers. Marketing brochures emphasized "very reasonable prices."[26]

Howard was able to sell his products for less, making them available to the masses, because he devised production techniques which were not labor intensive. Pottery must be made "quickly and easily in order to sell them at a reasonable price."[27] Painstaking hand labor makes products expensive.

Howard used porcelain, which could be finished with one firing, thereby doubling capacity. Howard's glaze procedures were quick and efficient compared to hand painting.

Time-consuming lines or products were soon discontinued, for example, the mugs, which required six pieces to cast, and the Wedgwood-like line. Dinnerware and large items, like jardinieres, were only made in small quantities as they took too much room in the kiln. Blue glazes were limited because cobalt was expensive, until his children gave him a quantity as a gift. For a short time, Howard incised his name on the bottom of pieces, but discontinued because of time.

A 1968 move to Joshua Tree, a desert community near Palm Springs, California, opened new horizons. Ten years earlier, they started coming to a cabin with five acres in Yucca Valley on weekends. With this decision to permanently establish a studio and home, the Pierces purchased a side of a mountain and created their own world. Just as the site, 20 acres above Joshua Tree, offered extraordinary views, vistas of creativity also broadened.

Photograph shows roof top of Pierce Joshua Tree home.

Strange, distinctive trees provided the town with its name. The Mormons designated these giant yuccas as Joshua trees "because of their upstretched 'arms'."[28] Joshua trees "with their shaggy bark resembling a pelt of rough fur and their controlled branches bearing clusters of spiny leaves — could hardly be imagined, but once seen, they can never be forgotten."[29]

Joshua Tree postcard.

Howard designed their new home and studio to nestle into the boulders and preserve the natural desert environment. Their home "blended in with the rocky scenery. The sidewalks and steps leading up to the house were made out of the surrounding stones. The natural landscaping was completed with jojoba plants and cacti to preserve water."[30]

Sidewalk and steps at Joshua Tree home.

A spectacular ornamental frieze adorned the house. Working for four months, Howard used latex molds to make the decorative horizontal band in two patterns — desert plant forms and a Northwest Native American motif.

Northwest Native American motif in ornamental frieze.

Decorative band with desert plant forms motif.

Desert flora and fauna were respected, enjoyed, and studied. Howard and Ellen Pierce lived in harmony and peace with the other forms of life in their world. Coyotes paid daily visits, coming to eat the dog food the Pierces mixed with hot water and spread out on the rocks. Some tamed coyotes would come within ten feet of them. Animals came all day to the drinking fountain Howard built for them outside the dining and living rooms. A family video showed rabbits, quail, roadrunners, and chipmunks drinking and eating. As a neighbor said, "You wouldn't believe the things you can see here. Animals come to see him."[31] Even the Joshua Tree address was appropriate — Cougar Lane.

Coyotes eating the dog food near the Pierce home.

Birds eating and drinking at the Pierce's.

Because Howard loved all God's creatures, snakes were allowed to use his fountain. "They need water and they're OK, just different."[32] However, he did kill poisonous snakes if they got too close to the house.

Howard trained a blue jay he named "BJ" to take food from him and others. BJ would also come into the studio and drink water from Howard's hand, which was dubbed the "St. Francis Act" by this family.

"BJ"

Ellen shared Howard's fascination with nature. She especially enjoyed the desert with its warmth and wide expanse. Today, Ellen continues to recall interesting tidbits of nature information and the names of trees, plants, animals, and birds.

The family had many pets over the years, including rats, Guinea pigs, and tadpoles. There were several family cats. "George," a special feline friend, kept Howard company during his final illness.

However, after they moved to the desert, they had no pets inside the house as they could "chase away wild animals."[33] Howard wanted to encourage the wild animals, whom he found "interesting to watch."[34]

Because he lived so closely with the desert birds and animals, Howard was able to get a feeling for the salient features of each. He would then emphasize that feature in his work, for example, the howling coyote.

With its prolonged drought, extreme heat, and radical temperature fluctuations, the desert is "one

Howard Pierce and kitten.

Broken molds.

of the harshest environments on earth."[35] However, "there is a varied plant and animal life, in many cases richer in actual numbers and variety than in much of our seemingly more flavored terrain."[36]

In this desert hideaway, Howard often focused on arid region inhabitants. He portrayed many of these birds and animals which have succeeded in adapting to their harsh habitat. From the Gambel quail to the prevalent roadrunner, jackrabbit, desert tortoise, and coyote, Pierce's figures described the desert. A local newspaper related that "a lot of people who come here take a piece of the desert, symbolized through his work, with them when they leave."[37]

After Howard suffered a mild stroke in November 1991, the Pierces decided to slow down and discontinue porcelain products. They had been going virtually nonstop since their marriage and "forty-eight years of watching a kiln is enough."[38] Word spread fast and they were sold out of stock in two weeks. Their children visited one weekend to help do the honors of breaking up all the old molds. Five pickup loads carried the breakage away.

Pierce worked in other media for a time but found he really missed porcelain. In 1993, Howard bought a small electric kiln and went back into production on a smaller scale. During this "second ceramics career,"[39] some of the pieces were created by making new molds over some of his original pieces. These pieces are a little smaller than the originals because the molds were made over the original pieces and firing causes some shrinkage. Others were new creations.

Howard with new kiln in 1993.

While very driven and productive, Howard Pierce was not reclusive in personality. One soon felt the genuine warmth and interest of this personable man. At once strong and gentle, his sense of humor and sharp wit often led to congenial bantering. When Howard retired, he said it was the people "he had met over the years through his artwork that he would miss."[40]

A highly motivated man, Pierce was not strongly influenced by external rewards. He made pottery for himself and for people to buy. No awards, no shows and no exhibitions for this man who "hated to be in front of people."[41]

When Howard was asked which of all the porcelain pieces he created was his favorite, he replied, "I don't know. I liked it all."[42] Linda described her father's favorite as "today's."[43] Ellen added, "He never dwelt on past things as he had new ones on his mind."[44]

Pierce was constantly experimenting. Almost every kiln contained experimental pieces. Thinking, planning, and making new things were the norm.

Persistent hard work was key to Howard's success. "The power of expression is not to be secured without labor. It cannot be expected that such a gift can be bestowed upon one who will give no price for it.... Clays are willful.... The art of manipulation is the outcome of long and arduous practice, and many failures must be faced before the ideal can be realized."[45]

Although plagued with medical problems toward the end of his life, he never let his health or anything else interfere with his work. Howard "thrived on hard work."[46] His hands were tough and strong, "made to work," as he affirmed. "I like to work with my hands."[47] Working 10 hour days throughout his pottery career, he followed a consistent routine, with "everyday planned to the minute."[48] Even in semi-retirement, Howard stated, "I'll work nine, ten hours a day. I've been doing that and it probably will stay that way."[49] "Pottery-making keeps me young."[50] Two weeks before he died on February 28, 1994, Howard Pierce was still designing and producing a polar bear model.

Extremely rare "Essence of Polar Bear." (Pierce Family Collection)

"Essence of Polar Bear" was Howard Pierce's last piece. The model was found after Howard died. His son, Jerry, made a mold over it and his children fired this final unglazed ware for family members.

PORCELAIN PROCESS

The vast majority of Howard Pierce's artistic creations were porcelain. In the process of making porcelain, high temperatures cause the clay body to fuse with the overlying glaze. This is known as vitrification — a glassy state resulting from the high firing which produces an extremely hard ware. A single firing of Pierce ware matured both the body and the glaze, vitrifying the clay into porcelain.

Howard Pierce used a clay body he formulated from China clay, ball clay, and potash feldspar. China clay is a primary clay which provides the white color desired in porcelain. Ball clay is used as a secondary clay because of its plasticity which improves working properties. Potash feldspar, which brings about vitrification by melting into glass, was also added to the composition.

Clay was Howard's favorite medium. "Working with clay is the best. It's more versatile than other materials, so you can do all kinds of things."[1] Charles Binns, considered the father of the American studio pottery movement, concurred, "Nothing can be more attractive than working with clay"[2] — "the facile plasticity which it possesses beyond and above any other substance."[3]

As an artisan, Howard Pierce appreciated the qualities of porcelain. As Binns states in *The Potters Craft*, "The production of porcelain is the goal of the potter. The pure white of the clay and the possibility of employing high temperatures exert a profound influence upon the imagination while the difficulties of manipulation only serve to stimulate the energy of the enthusiast."[4] A practical man, Howard also preferred porcelain's strength, durability, and ability to hold water.

Ideas for his porcelains came easily to Howard Pierce. Sometimes, Pierce would just "catch ideas."[5] For example, he might see something in nature or build upon a concept he observed. Ellen and his family also offered ideas.

Two file drawers overflowed with photos, clippings, and sketches from magazines, papers, and books, which family members found and gave him. When creating new pieces, Howard would spread out the pertinent resources and first sketch from these or nature.

Using his drawings, Howard then molded the sculpture in clay and made a mold from this model. Howard Pierce porcelains were all produced using molds.

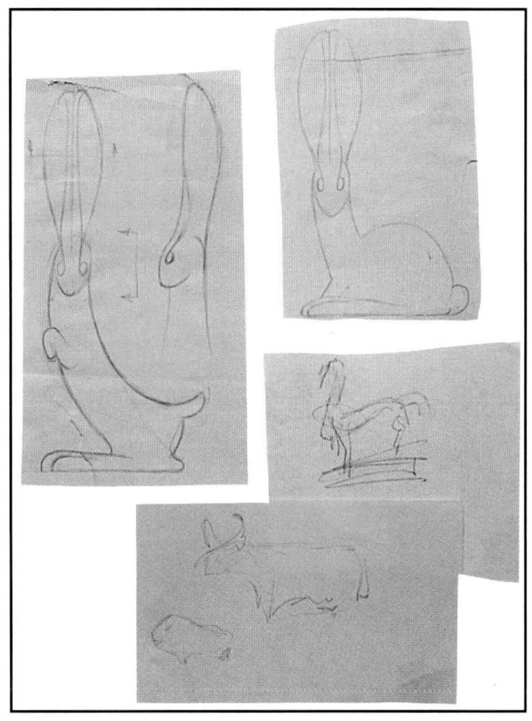

Howard Pierce sketches.

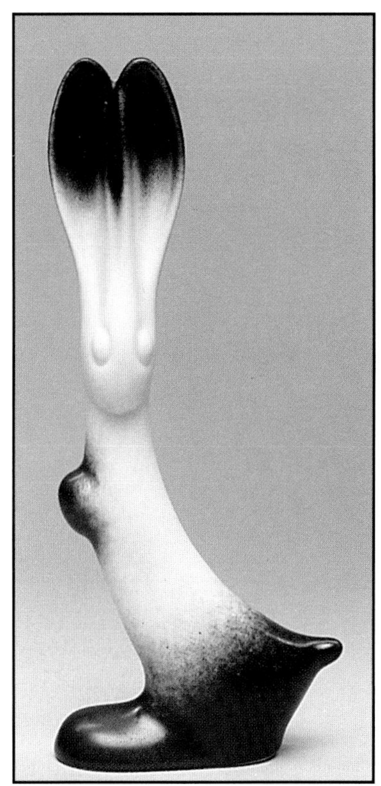

Porcelain jackrabbit resulting from sketches, 10½" x 4¾", "Howard Pierce" impressed into mold and mold number/letter combination "102P," $75.00 –100.00.

Molding or casting followed a standard process — slip was poured into the mold and excess was poured out after some water had been absorbed by the mold, forming the piece. The greenware was taken from the mold and allowed to set and harden. When not completely dry, the seam line was trimmed with a knife. When thoroughly dry, the whole piece was sponged with an natural sponge.

View from studio.

Howard working with molds.

All decorating was done by spray glazing the greenware before firing. Using a hand-held spray gun containing about a quart of glaze, Howard applied the undercoat in a background color first. Some areas were left unsprayed where a white final color was wanted. Then he sprayed the whole piece with a white coat. This second white glaze was wiped off with a brush to the first dark coat, creating accents. Howard added CMC powder as an ingredient to the first layer of a glaze if he wanted to apply spray on top of it and be able to wipe some of the top layer off without wiping off both layers.[6] Areas with no dark base coat came out as pure white. Areas covered with both the dark and white glazes fired as brownish because the dark color bubbled up through the white. Areas where the white was wiped off, like eyes, ears, and tails, turned out almost black. Describing his unique glaze procedure, Howard stated, "We are the only ones I know who have come out with items that look hand painted but are actually sprayed."[7] "When the glaze is wiped off it blends in, doesn't look painted and is quick to do."[8]

Greenware ready for glazing.

Howard in spray booth.

Glazing.

Considered a "salient aspect of the work," Howard Pierce's glazes made his porcelains unique. Howard developed all his own formulas, making the glazes from scratch, using materials purchased from Westwood Ceramic Supply, City of Industry, California. The Pierce glazes were difficult for competitors to copy. As Ellen stated, some unusual glazes were "one-of-a-kind" and even Howard couldn't replicate them.

Howard did all his own glaze application, except when training Linda one summer. Constantly changing glazes, Howard for years experimented with many "test" glazes, including one in each kiln fired.

Satin-matte white was Howard's earliest glaze color, followed by satin-matte brown on white, his "favorite finish for almost fifteen years."[9] Advertising brochures of the 50s list three satin-matte glazes — brown on white, black on white, and all black. Other basic colors included matte white, matte brown, matte gray on white, gloss black, gloss white, gloss brown, sea green, and red. Later, gray gloss and matte brown granite with texture were added.

Several other special or experimental colors or combinations were used over time, including dark green gloss, light pink, lime green, salmon, Wedgwood blue, and speckled green, red, and black.

In the late 1970s, Howard incised numbers in the clay of experimental or test products. With the numbering system, glazes could be successfully recreated. Colors used on these experimental pieces included blues, deep greens, black, purples, pinks, and yellows.

Howard Pierce's unique lava glaze had nothing to do with actual lava or ash. To get the effect of "bubbling up from the bottom,"[10] Howard used manganese dioxide in the body. Since results were unpredictable, little was made for the commercial market.

After friends sent some volcanic ash from the 1980 eruption of Mount St. Helens, Howard created a volcanic ash glaze. Ash gathered at different distances from St. Helens created color variations in the final products. The rough textured glaze was soon discontinued as it jammed and ruined Howard's spray gun. Pieces were marked with "St. Helens" hand printed in black ink and the standard "HOWARD PIERCE" black ink stamp.

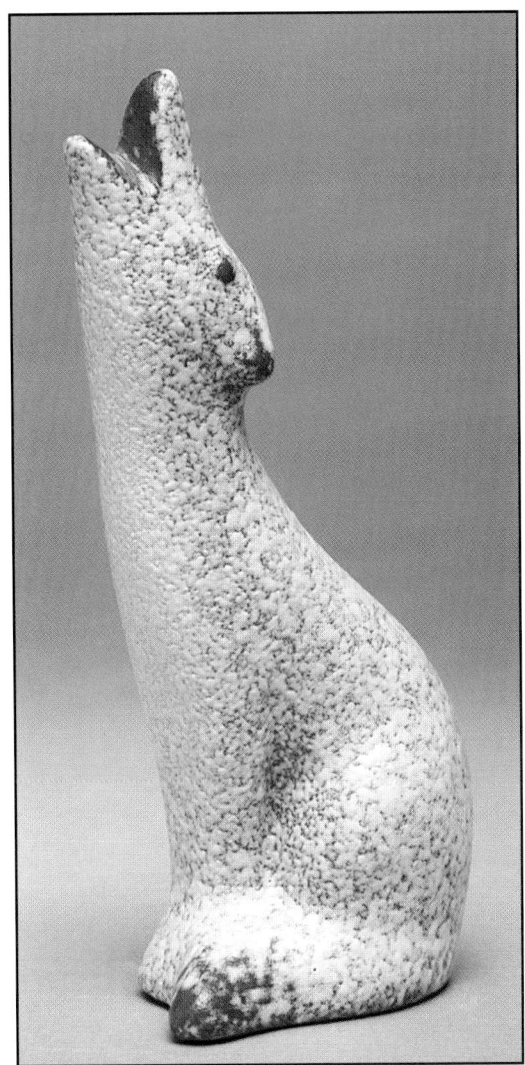

Highly textured lava glaze coyote, $5\frac{3}{4}$" x $2\frac{3}{4}$", black ink stamp "HOWARD PIERCE" with "Pierce" hand signed in black ink and experimental number "K70," $75.00 – 100.00.

Two $6\frac{1}{2}$" long hippos, with volcanic ash glaze, "St. Helens" handwritten in black ink and black ink stamp "HOWARD PIERCE," $75.00 – 100.00 each. (Pierce Family Collection)

Although it was "impossible for Pierce to track how many pieces of his ceramics have been made,"[1] the ware was limited. Even though Howard Pierce produced for over 50 years, his enterprise remained the small, home-based business of a sole studio potter.

Because of the porcelain durability and glaze quality, the collector seldom finds firing or damage flaws in Pierce porcelain ware. Problems like chipping, cracking, crazing, pitting, bubbles, glaze skips, and blistering are infrequent or non-existent.

Seconds were not marked as such. Howard kept a special shelf of these pieces in his studio and would either sell them at a discount or give them away. He used others for target practice, "to shoot their heads off,"[2] and was very accurate.

Molds were destroyed throughout the pottery's history. Whenever the Pierces were finished with them because of wear or sales decline, they broke the molds. In 1992, when porcelain production ceased, the Pierces also ended an era by destroying the molds. This protected the collector as they could not be reused by someone else in the future.[3]

Some Pierce creations are cross-over collectibles, those sought by more than one group of collectors. For example, a Howard Pierce turtle bank may appeal to bank collectors or turtle collectors as well as collectors of Howard Pierce memorabilia. Many other Howard Pierce items, including dogs, cats, horses, whistles, and magnets are cross-over collectibles.

Not only an artist, but also a market-oriented entrepreneur, Howard Pierce sought to create what was desired by the public. In order to "reach an ever-increasing number of people...common denominations taste must be the rule in design."[4] Thus, Pierce ware reflects the era. Even the popular colors of the time are represented, for example chartreuse of the 50s.

Today, collectors are turning back to the 50s and 60s with renewed interest. Pierce porcelains again find their niche in homes and lifestyles.

Howard Pierce's work found its way to all states and several countries. The Pierces benefited from the strong tourist trade which California enjoyed then and now. Nationwide distribution systems also promoted the ware throughout the country.

From 1950 to 1966, the Pierces used a wholesaler for marketing their ware. N. S. Gustin, Los Angeles, provided nationwide distribution to many gift shops and some major upscale department stores, like Macy's, Neiman Marcus, Marshall Field's, Frederick-Nelson, and Bullocks, as well as their centers at the Chicago Merchandise Mart and Showcase New York (Appendix). Most orders were placed at the Los Angeles show in August, for Christmas delivery, and at the spring show. It was especially beneficial at this time "to market wares aggressively in the populous East."[5] Mr. Gustin controlled the quality of merchandise and regulated quantities produced. Howard felt that Gustin was "as fair as any man I ever deal with."[6] This business relationship proved to be very successful.

A few wholesale accounts were maintained like Casa Flores, a Claremont florist/gift shop. The Frankoma Pottery Gift Shop, Sapulpa, Oklahoma, sold Pierce products for years to supplement their own lines. At one time, Joniece Frank wanted to buy Howard's molds but he refused to sell any. He didn't want anyone else to use his designs. Another wholesale account was Calico Ghost Town, Barstow, California, a restored 1880s mining town. Pierce porcelain was sold in the pottery gift shop.

After moving to Joshua Tree, the Pierces continued to deal with N. S. Gustin for several years and also sold locally through the hospital and museum gift shops. Ellen stated that Howard never took to selling at fairs or shows. They also sold directly from their home studio. For awhile, they shipped UPS but then stopped all retail mail order as the boxes got too heavy to handle. Visitors were welcome at the studio, by appointment. They continued to be able to sell all they produced. As Howard said, there was "no reason for"[7] other merchandising methods.

Howard with inventory at studio.

The majority of Howard Pierce porcelains are marked. Many of the marks are shown and described here. However, other variations also exist. No record was kept of all marks used or years of usage, according to Ellen Pierce.

• The standard mark, used through most years of production, was a black or brown ink stamped full name in block letters, " HOWARD PIERCE." This mark appears either under the glaze or on bisque.

• In the 50s, the word "PORCELAIN" was added to "HOWARD PIERCE," emphasizing this quality material. The word was dropped after a short time.

• "Claremont, Calif," along with "Howard Pierce," all in script under the glaze, were incised into the mold on two or four lines during the Claremont era. Family members stated that location was added to show United States production as the ware was sold in Canada.

• Howard sometimes added his name and/or date in ink, when pieces were purchased at his studio or on special orders.

Howard signing pieces.

•Stock number/letter combinations, impressed into the mold and under the glaze, were used on some early items.

•Experimental glaze number/letter combinations of later years were handwritten or incised and not under the glaze.

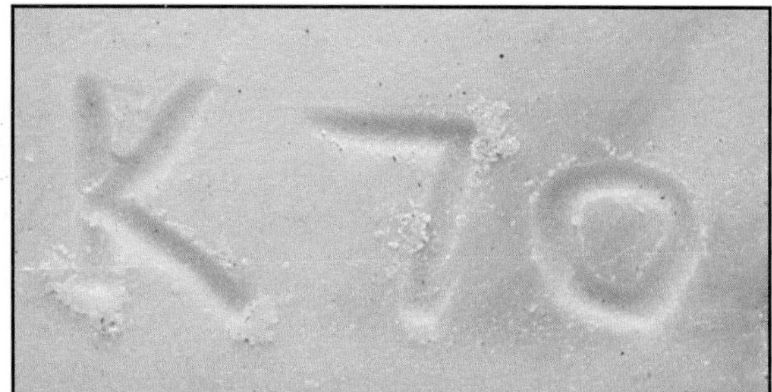

•Other marks

Impressed into mold with block letters.

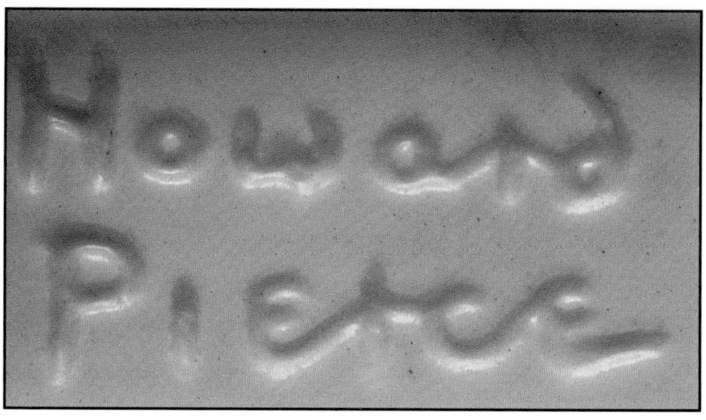

Impressed into mold in script.

Impressed into mold with copyright notice in script.

Brown ink stamp in block letters with copyright notice.

Initials incised into mold by hand, used on limited number of pieces.

Mark handwritten in ink on the piece.

Black ink stamp in block letters.

Incised by hand in script, sometimes with date.

In groups of two or three, usually only one piece was marked, most commonly the largest one. Therefore, unmarked pieces may be found.

With their distinctive style, Pierce porcelains "jump out at you" when seen with other pottery and collectibles. Therefore, a collector familiar with Pierce examples, can easily recognize unmarked Pierce ware.

The bottoms of the set of three giraffes with only the largest of the set marked.

When subject matter deals with natural images, like animals and birds, examples from different potteries may appear somewhat alike because of the innate nature of the living specimen. For example, a quail by Howard Pierce may look somewhat like a quail by Roselane. Ellen stated that the Japanese tried to copy Pierce porcelains without much success.

Stanford Pottery of Sebring, Ohio, is often mistaken for Howard Pierce ware because of the glaze color and shapes. The geese are an example. Several differences exist. Stanford glaze is often poorly applied, and some shape details, like goose beaks, differ. Also, Stanford bases have larger bottom holes, being cut almost to the edge. These large holes in the Stanford goose bases made marking difficult. Howard Pierce pieces and Stanford planters are usually marked.

Stanford Pottery, two geese, 8½" x 7¼", unmarked, $20.00 – 25.00 pair. Note different beak shape. Planter, 5½" x 8", marked "Stanford Sebring O.," $15.00 – 20.00.

Howard Pierce gaggle of geese, 7½" x 5½" goose, unmarked; 5¼" x 6" goose, unmarked; 8½" x 6" gander, "PIERCE" impressed into mold and stock letter/number combination "23 OP," $75.00 – 100.00 set.

PRODUCT LINES

Production of dinnerware, such as bowls, plates, serving dishes, and sugars and creamers, was mainly for the Pierce family. All dinnerware was porcelain, fired to 2,150° F. According to Linda, dinnerware was not mass produced or distributed through the Gustin Company. However, a small quantity was sold to the public out of the studio salesroom.

2" sugar and creamer with white gloss glaze flowing over maroon, "HOWARD PIERCE PORCELAIN" impressed into mold and stock number/letter combination "1XS," $85.00 – 100.00 set. (Pierce Family Collection)

5" triangular gray dish, unmarked, $60.00 – 75.00; 3¾" square gray dish, "HOWARD PIERCE" impressed into mold and stock number/letter combination "P-2," $50.00 – 65.00; 8" triangular tan dish, unmarked, $75.00 – 85.00. (Pierce Family Collection)

Triangular gray dishes, 16" x 12" and 10" x 5¼", both unmarked, $85.00 – 100.00 and $75.00 – 85.00. (Pierce Family Collection)

An appealing line of high gloss vases and planters with open centers was created at Claremont. Miniature porcelain bisque or high gloss white plant and animal forms adorned the open areas or were placed on side shelves. These miniatures were made of the same Jasperware-type body used in the cameos. The line was short-lived due to poor salability and the amount of labor involved.

Three high gloss planters with white bisque horses and trees, forest green, white, and chartreuse, called "celadon green" by the family, each 7" x 9$^{1}/_{4}$", "Howard Pierce Claremont, Calif." impressed into each mold and "HP 500" stock number/letter combination on white one, $85.00 – 100.00 each.

Howard working on bisque plant form in Claremont studio.

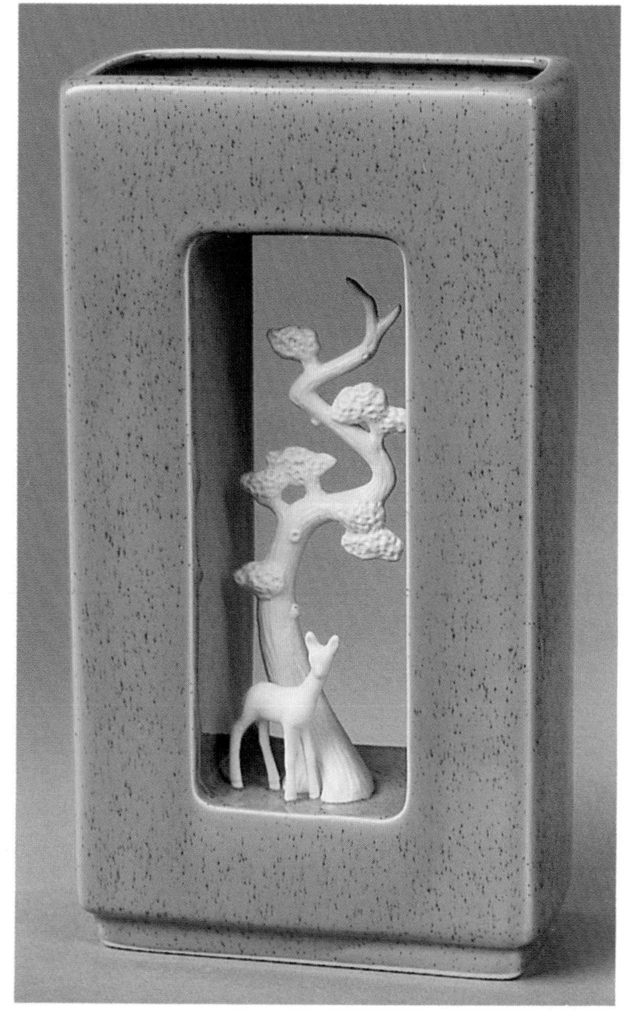

Gray high gloss planter with white bisque deer and tree, 4$^{3}/_{4}$" x 9", "Howard Pierce Claremont, Calif." impressed into mold and stock number/letter combination "30P," $100.00 –125.00.

Chartreuse high gloss vase with bisque fawn and tree, 11$^{1}/_{2}$" x 6", "Howard Pierce Claremont Calif." impressed into clay, $85.00 – 100.00.

Dark green and chartreuse 9" x $5^{3}/_{4}$" vases with flamingo and giraffe bisque, both marked "Howard Pierce Claremont Calif." impressed into clay, $85.00 – 100.00 each.

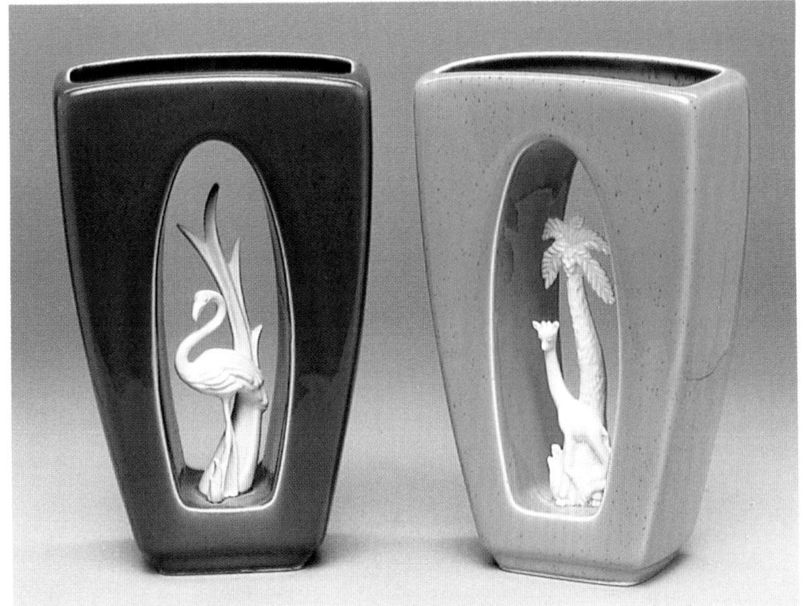

Two $5^{1}/_{4}$" x $6^{1}/_{4}$" high gloss glaze vases, dark green with girl walking dog insert and white with insert of boy and dog, "Howard Pierce Claremont Calif." impressed into mold of both, $85.00 – 100.00 each. (Ron and Juvelyn Nickel Collection)

Green high gloss glaze 8" x 7" vase with white fish insert, "Howard Pierce Claremont Calif." impressed into mold, $100.00 – 125.00. (Ron and Juvelyn Nickel Collection)

Deer and tree on black base beside white high gloss vase, 7$^{1}/_{2}$" x 5", "Howard Pierce Claremont Calif." impressed into mold, $85.00 – 100.00. (Ron and Juvelyn Nickel Collection)

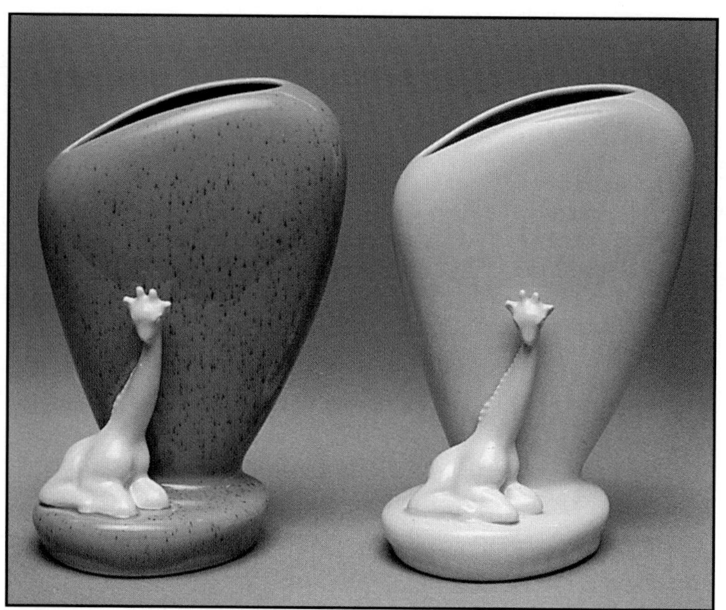

Chartreuse high gloss vase and white high gloss vase, both with white high gloss giraffes nestled into sides, both 7$^{1}/_{4}$" x 4", "Howard Pierce" impressed into mold and stock number/letter combination "250 P," $85.00 – 100.00 each.

Green high gloss planter with white gloss glaze deer nestled into side, 2$^{1}/_{2}$" x 10", "Howard Pierce Claremont, Calif." impressed into mold and stock number/letter combination "80P," $85.00 – 100.00.

In the 1940s, Howard Pierce developed ware he called "Wedgwood-like," his own version of Wedgwood's Jasperware. Josiah Wedgwood first produced Jasper in 1774 at his English pottery. This ware became "synonymous with the name Wedgwood."[1] The dense, vitrified stoneware of Jasper is "fired with relief decoration in another color in order to achieve a cameo effect."[2]

Jasperware was stoneware in contrast to porcelain. Although both vitrify in the kiln, stoneware is made from clays which can fire to colors other than pure white, with a matte appearance. Porcelain is a glazed ware which fires to white translucent ware.

Wedgwood's solid Jasper was never glazed and a tint throughout the clay body attempted to "imitate natural cameos."[3] Natural cameos are gems or stones "engraved in relief, especially with layers of different hues, cut so the raised design is one color and the background another."[4] Wedgwood Jasper dip, a less expensive ware that was dipped in a colored Jasper slip, was introduced later in 1785.

Wedgwood relief decorations were fired separately in molds. The reliefs were then dampened on the undercoated side with water and carefully positioned onto the background piece.

Howard's ware exhibits some characteristics similar to Wedgwood, being unglazed and using relief decorations in other colors. Howard used the solid jasper process, tinting the clay throughout the body, but a different process for the reliefs.

Ellen described the difficult and delicate labor-intensive procedure of producing the relief decorations. The relief figures were actually part of the mold and not added afterwards. Color was added afterwards in a process Howard developed.[5] Production was short-lived due to the expense of this labor-intensive process.

Pale blue Art Deco vase, 6" x 6", "Howard Pierce Claremont, Calif." impressed into mold and stock number/letter combination "70F," $100.00 – 125.00. (Pierce Family Collection)

Art Deco, a term coined in honor of the 1925 Exposition Internationale des Arts Decoratifs et Industriels Modernes in Paris as a stylistic movement, emphasized "streamlined, functional, abstract design."[6]

Pale blue Art Deco gazelle planter, $2^1/_2$" x $9^3/_4$", "Howard Pierce Claremont Calif." impressed into mold, $100.00 – 125.00. (Pierce Family Collection)

Leaping gazelles, "proverbial for their beauty and speed,"[7] were a "recurrent feature of Art Deco," such as the Gazelle Bowl of 1935, designed for Steuben Glass by Sidney Waugh.[8]

Mint green lidded box with Art Deco gazelles, 4" x 5", "Howard Pierce Claremont Calif." impressed into mold, $125.00 – 150.00 (Pierce Family Collection)

6" pale blue teapot of shepherd with sheep, "Howard Pierce Claremont Calif." impressed into mold, set of teapot, sugar, and creamer (page 30), $150.00 – 200.00. (Pierce Family Collection)

2$^{3}/_{4}$" pale blue sugar and creamer with lamb motif on each side, "Howard Pierce" impressed into mold, set of teapot, sugar, and creamer, $150.00 – 200.00. The Gustin Company distributed these at one time. (Pierce Family Collection)

Three Wedgwood-type vases with white cameos on deep blue circles and pale blue backgrounds. Oriental boy on 5$^{3}/_{4}$" x 5$^{1}/_{2}$" vase, impressed into mold "Howard Pierce Claremont Calif."; girl with flowers on 4" diameter vase, impressed into mold "Howard Pierce Claremont Calif."; and girl with umbrella and basket on 5$^{3}/_{4}$" x 5$^{1}/_{2}$" vase, impressed into mold "Howard Pierce." $75.00 – 100.00 each. (Ron and Juvelyn Nickel Collection)

Sheep and shepherd pale blue sugar/creamer set, 4$^{1}/_{4}$", mark impressed into mold in script, "Howard Pierce Claremont Calif.," $100.00 – 125.00 set; salmon-colored fish motif vase, 4$^{1}/_{4}$", mark impressed into mold, "HOWARD PIERCE," $75.00 – 100.00. (Pierce Family Collection)

Mint green matte glaze planter with leaf motif, 2¼" x 6¾", "Howard Pierce Claremont Calif." impressed into clay and mold number/letter combination "80P," $50.00 – 75.00.

Mint green matte glaze planter with leaf motif, 4¼" x 6½", "Howard Pierce Claremont Calif." impressed into mold, $50.00 – 75.00.

Mint green leaf planter, 7" x 9½", mark impressed into clay in script "Howard Pierce Claremont Calif." and stock number/letter combination "82P" impressed into mold, $50.00 – 75.00. (Pierce Family Collection)

Mint green leaf vases, 6" x $5^{1}/_{2}$" and 5" x $4^{3}/_{4}$", both with "Howard Pierce Claremont Calif." impressed into mold, \$50.00 – 75.00 each.

Gray wall pocket, $2^{1}/_{4}$" x $5^{1}/_{2}$", "Howard Pierce Claremont Calif." impressed into mold, and stock number/letter combination "42P," \$75.00 – 100.00.

Two matte salmon-colored flower pots, $4^{1}/_{4}$" x $4^{1}/_{4}$", "Howard Pierce Claremont Calif." impressed into mold and stock number/letter combination "81P"; center matte salmon-colored vase, 6" x $5^{1}/_{2}$", "Howard Pierce Claremont Calif." impressed into mold. \$50.00 – 75.00 each.

Following a 1950s suggestion of a Pomona company, Howard produced ware for a gold line. After designing the shapes or using molds he already had, Howard made the cast bisque pieces. The rest of the process, beyond the casting, was all contracted out to others, according to family members. Howard made a few himself for testing and taught Linda the process. Early pieces were contracted out to a business in Pomona. Later, those done in the desert, were done by couples taught by Howard.[9]

Linda and Howard gold leafing.

5½" vase with owls, "PIERCE" impressed into mold, $50.00 – 75.00. To achieve highlights, some pieces were brushed with oil paint — burnt amber or burnt sienna — which was then rubbed off with a cloth as a final procedure.

Historically, when creating gold leaf, the gold material was placed on top of a red background. Therefore, in an attempt to look authentic, Pierce bisque was painted with red paint and very thin gold plastic from Germany was applied over a coating of glue. Howard's procedure then involved rubbing the piece with sheepskin, allowing it to dry overnight and spraying with clear enamel.[10]

Perhaps those gold leafed by others were not sprayed with the clear enamel as the gold easily peeled, revealing the red undercoat. However, gold pieces in the Pierce family collection, completely made by Howard, are still in mint condition. Most gold pieces are unmarked.

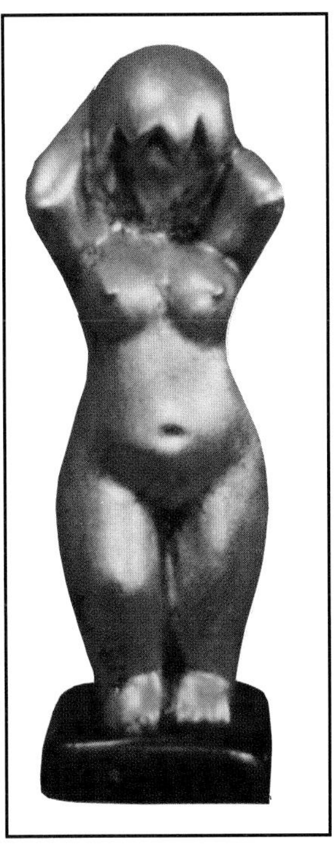

Rare 9" nude figure, unmarked, $250.00+. (Pierce Family Collection)

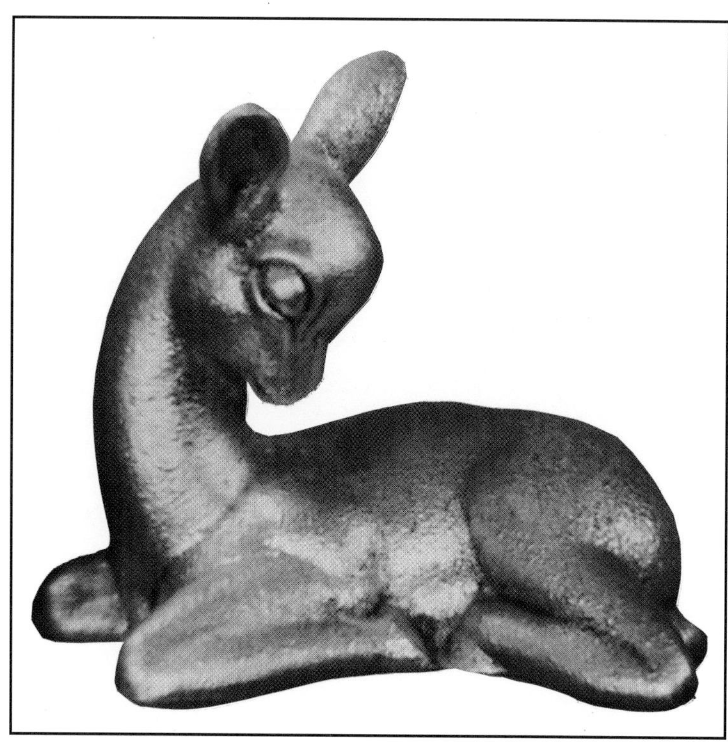

Rare 12" deer, unmarked, $250.00+. (Pierce Family Collection)

Howard Pierce's version of "The Beatles," rare one-of-a-kind set, made for his family, 9", 10", and 7", unmarked, $350.00+. (Pierce Family Collection)

Rare 14" giraffe, unmarked, $250.00+. (Pierce Family Collection)

9" bird, unmarked, \$35.00 – 50.00; two quail in tree, 9" x 3¼", unmarked, \$60.00 – 75.00; 5¾" x 4¾" bird, unmarked, \$35.00 – 50.00. All have gold overglaze with red occasionally showing through.

2½" x 5½" gold bird, unmarked, \$35.00 – 50.00.

Rare optometrist set, 9½", 4½", and 6½", marked "Pierce" in black ink. Howard created this set for his own optometrist. The gleeful optomtrist anticipates his two potential patients, near-sighted and far-sighted. He made two sets — one in white glaze for the optometrist and this one to keep, \$350.00+. (Pierce Family Collection)

PORCELAIN PRODUCTS

Signs

Dealer's 2½" x 6½" sign, brown rough surface, similar to tree bark, black ink stamp "HOWARD PIERCE" and handwritten "Pierce" in black ink, $125.00 – 150.00.

According to Ellen, the sign was given to dealers who sold Pierce products in some quantity. For a limited time one year, a brown glaze dealer sign, like the one pictured above, was advertised for sale by the *American Clay Exchange* as a service to the magazine's readers.

Another dealer's sign was made earlier. The rare 2½" x 6" sign read "PIERCE" at the top in 1½" letters with "PORCELAIN" underneath in ½" letters.

First and second edition 3" x 6" signs commemorating the 1985 and 1986 California pottery shows at Glendale, California, made in experimental colors and marked "Howard Pierce" and "Limited Edition" in the mold on the back, $75.00 – 100.00 each. (Ron and Juvelyn Nickel Collection)

Cross-Over Collectibles

The only whistle Howard designed, a bird, was tricky to make. After the bird was sprayed, a hole had to be cut into the back by hand at just the correct angle. Otherwise, the whistle wouldn't work.

2¾" x 2" bird whistle, black ink stamp "HOWARD PIERCE," $100.00 –125.00.

A series of banks included a bear, pig, hippopotamus, and turtle. Limited numbers were made as buyers were unwilling to pay extra for the required extra time necessary to cut the hole. Howard viewed the bank as mainly a child's piece, feeling that making a figurine into a bank distracted from the artistic creation.[1]

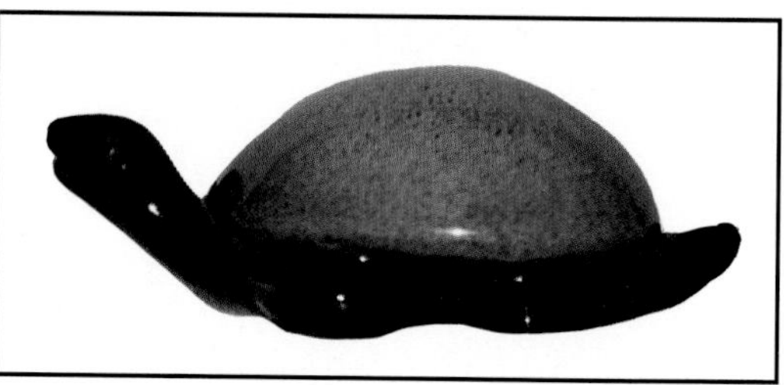

Turtle bank, 3" x 8", black high gloss body and green high gloss shell, black ink stamp "HOWARD PIERCE PORCELAIN," $150.00 – 175.00. (Ron and Juvelyn Nickel Collection)

3" brown mug, marked with initials "HP" incised into mold, $50.00 – 65.00; 7" coyote with "FORT IRWIN" incised into side, black ink stamp "HOWARD PIERCE," and handwritten in black ink "Pierce 1991", $75.00 – 85.00; rare 5¾" vase with incised hearts, gift from Howard to Ellen, $150.00+; rare pig bank with brown mottled glaze flowing down over solid brown at base, 4" x 7", black ink stamp "HOWARD PIERCE," $175.00; two rare 2½" eyewash cups made for Ellen's eye cup collection, unmarked, $125.00+ each; 3" roadrunner mug, marked with initials "HP" incised into mold, $100.00 – 125.00. (Pierce Family Collection)

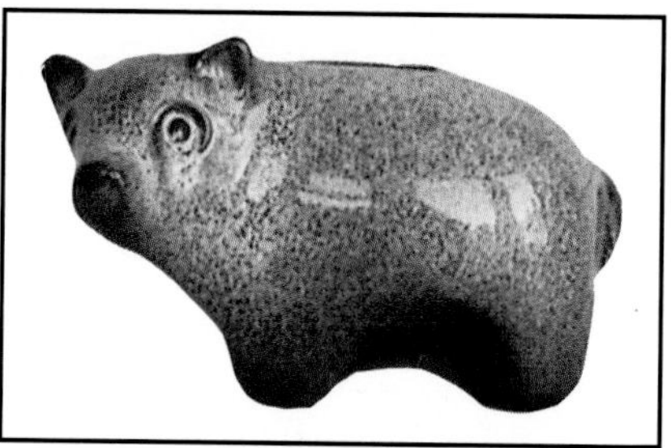

4" x 7" pig bank with high gloss brownish gray glaze, black ink stamp "HOWARD PIERCE," $150.00 – 175.00. (Bob and Clara Sweet Collection)

$3^{1}/_{4}$" rabbit magnet, unmarked, $50.00 – 75.00.

$5^{1}/_{2}$" coyote magnet on base, unmarked, $50.00 – 75.00.

Variety of magnets, unmarked, $50.00 – 75.00. (Pierce Family Collection)

Dogs are the most popular pet worldwide, with over 50 million in the United States. The domestic dog, which has worked, played, and endured with man for a hundred centuries, has been considered magical and ineffable, "that which is beyond explanation or description."[2] A resilient and adaptable creature, "above all it is a sociable beast."[3]

Since the dog "holds a unique position in human society,"[4] great interest in dog collectibles is understandable.

Howard Pierce made only a few dog figurine shapes. Pierce felt that people wouldn't buy dog figures unless they were the same breeds as their own dogs.

Pair of dogs with drooping ears, 8" x 3", "HOWARD PIERCE" black ink stamp, and 6" x 2½", unmarked, $85.00 – 125.00 set.

Generic dog with long ears, 6¾" x 3", "HOWARD PIERCE" black ink stamp, $65.00 – 75.00.

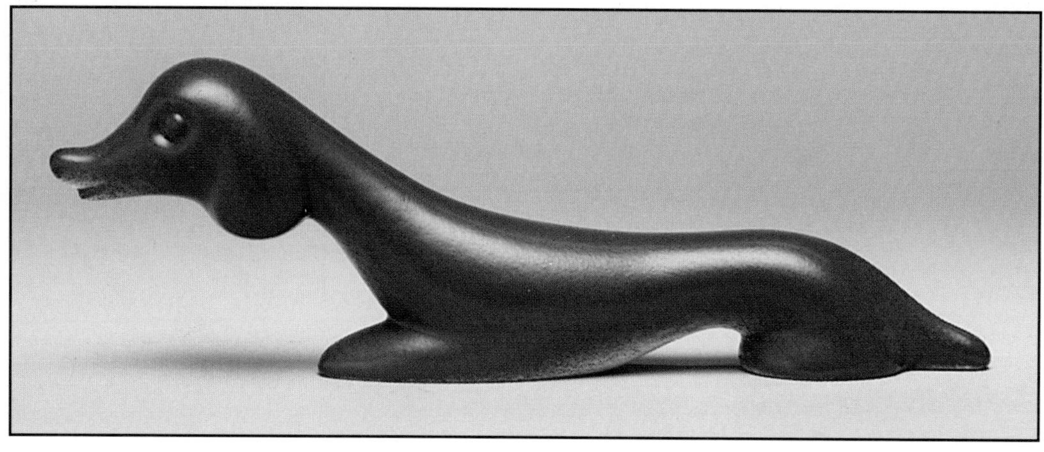

Dachshund, 3¼" x 10", "HOWARD PIERCE" black ink stamp, $85.00 –100.00.

Cats are America's favorite pets with over five million more cats than dogs living in U. S. households. Since the ancient Egyptian pharaohs, who revered the domesticated cat before 1900 B. C., the cat has been chronicled in history.

Feline fanciers eagerly seek collectibles of this much-loved animal, which "conjures up in each of our minds our own secret image. Above all, the cat leaves man with a sense of the unknown and mystery."[5]

With the feline image a constant world-wide artists' subject, Howard Pierce also sought "to capture the cat's elusive soul."[6] Since "Cat collectors don't seem to be as particular about breeds as dog collectors,"[7] the "generic cat" would sell. Pierce created many cats.

Pair of cats with white to grayish high gloss glaze, 5½" x 2¾" and 3¼" x 5", both marked with "HOWARD PIERCE" black ink stamp and handwritten "Pierce" in black ink, $100.00 – 125.00 pair.

Black 10¼", gray 10¼", and white 8½" cats, black ink stamp "HOWARD PIERCE," $60.00 –75.00 each. (Pierce Family Collection)

4" pair of black cats on base used as an illustration on cover of *Colliers* Magazine, signed "Pierce 1965" by hand in black ink, $125.00 – 150.00. (Pierce Family Collection)

Pair of cats, 4¾" x 4½" and 5½" x 3¼", both unmarked, $85.00 - 100.00 pair.

Black high gloss glaze slant-eye cat, 8" x 3", "HOWARD PIERCE" black ink stamp, $60.00 – 75.00.

Three cats, $10^{1}/_{4}$" x $3^{1}/_{2}$" and two other 8" x 3", all marked with "HOWARD PIERCE" black ink stamp, small cats $60.00 – 75.00 each, large cat $75.00 – 90.00.

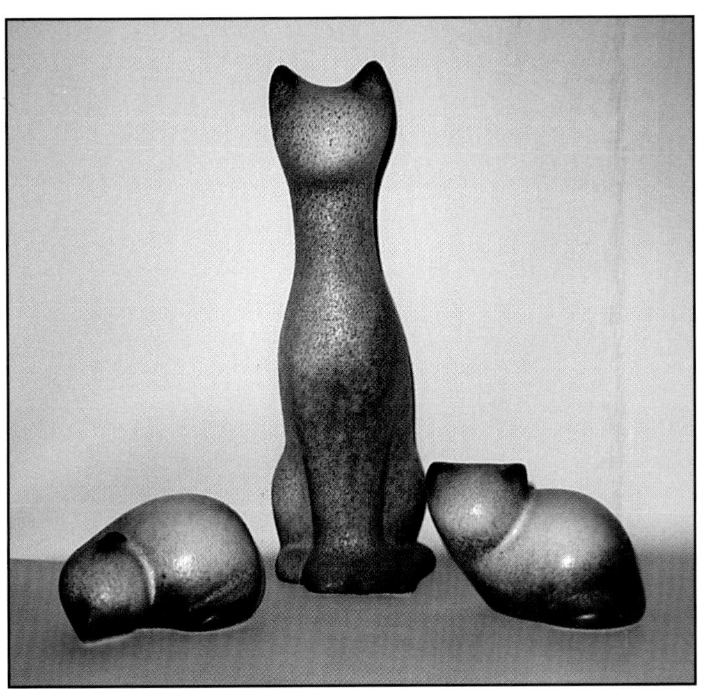

Group of faceless cats, all marked with black ink stamp "HOWARD PIERCE," pair of small cats, 2" x 4" and 3" x 4", $175.00 – 200.00 pair; 11" x $4^{1}/_{2}$" tall cat, $150.00 – 175.00. (Ron and Juvelyn Nickel Collection)

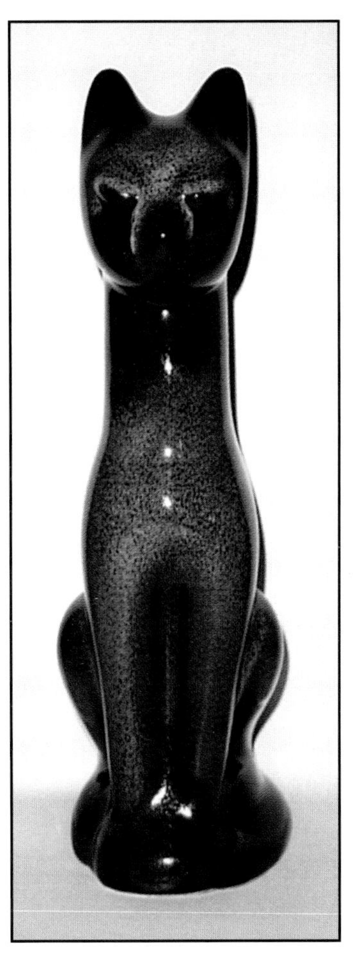

14" x 6" cat with striking bluish-black glaze, "Howard Pierce Clarmont Calif." impressed into mold, $250.00 – 275.00. (Ron and Juvelyn Nickel Collection)

With a domesticated history going back to as early as 5,000 B. C., the horse has long been a friend to mankind. "The scope of equine collectibles is very wide,"[8] as increasing numbers of horse lovers seek memorabilia.

Rare maroon base horse, 8½" x 10", black ink stamp "HOWARD PIERCE PORCELAIN," $500.00+; white horse on carousel-type base, 6¼" x 7½", marked with black ink stamp "HOWARD PIERCE" and by hand in black ink "Pierce 1990 3/7/90"; blue horse on base, 6¼" x 7½", brown ink stamp "HOWARD PIERCE" and black ink "Pierce 1989," $100.00 – 150.00 each. (Pierce Family Collection)

8" x 10" horse, black ink stamp "HOWARD PIERCE PORCELAIN," $250.00 – 275.00.

Horse with flying mane, 8½" x 7½", black ink stamp "HOWARD PIERCE," $125.00 – 150.00. (Bob and Clara Sweet Collection)

Wildlife

Enjoyment of wildlife is universal, a reminder "that we share our planet Earth with a huge number of other creatures. The very wildness also attracts us. There is something special about animals that are wild and free — that don't depend on humans and still live as they have for thousands or even millions of years."[9]

Rare elephant waterfall, 12" x 8", black ink stamp "HOWARD PIERCE," $500.00+. This elephant waterfall is a good example of Howard's skill as a gifted mold maker. He designed and made a ceramic pump so that water poured from the elephant's trunk. Only one was made as the complicated mold made it too expensive and it would need to be sold with the pumping mechanism. (Pierce Family Collection)

Howard with bison.

Rare pink elephant, 4½" x 4", black ink stamp "HOWARD PIERCE," $200.00+. (Ron and Juvelyn Nickel Collection)

Elephants both 6" x 3", greenish brown marked with black ink stamp "HOWARD PIERCE," "1984" handwritten in black ink and experimental number "A16" handwritten, $75.00 – 100.00; lava glaze elephant with "HOWARD PIERCE" brown ink stamp and experimental mark "BR05," $75.00 – 100.00; deer, 5¾" x 4½", "HOWARD PIERCE" black ink stamp and experimental number "S49," $50.00 – 65.00; polar bear, 3½" x 7", "HOWARD PIERCE" black ink stamp, $125.00 – 150.00; rare rhinoceros 3½" x 6¼", marked "Pierce 1992" in black ink by hand, $200.00+; white 2¾" unmarked bear, $40.00 – 50.00. (Pierce Family Collection)

Fawn, 3" x 4", unmarked, and doe 5¾" x 5", "HOWARD PIERCE" black ink stamp, $75.00 – 100.00 set.

Large 6½" x 8" fawn, black ink stamp "HOWARD PIERCE," $125.00 – 150.00. (Ron and Juvelyn Nickel Collection)

Brown high gloss glaze gazelle on base, $11^{1}/_{4}$" x 4", "Howard Pierce" impressed into mold and "100P," $100.00 – 125.00.

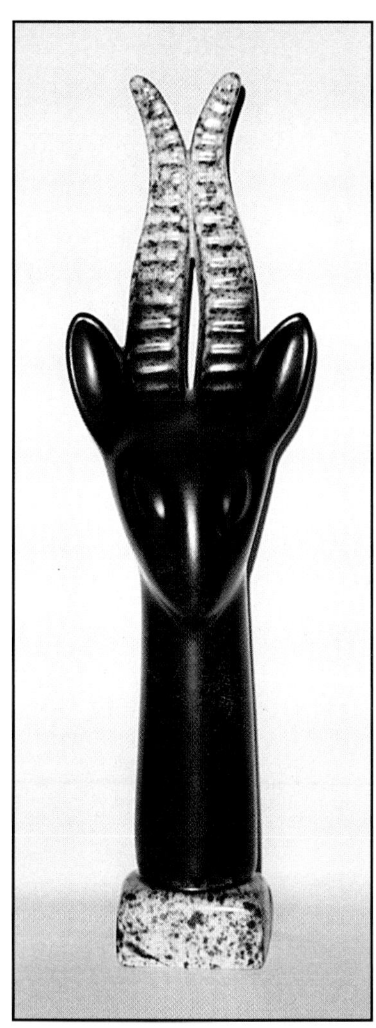

Rare gazelle head, $16^{1}/_{2}$" x 5", black ink stamp "HOWARD PIERCE," $250.00+. (Ron and Juvelyn Nickel Collection)

Three black matte giraffes, $11^{1}/_{2}$" x $2^{3}/_{4}$", black ink stamp "HOWARD PIERCE"; $5^{1}/_{2}$" x $1^{3}/_{4}$", unmarked; and $9^{1}/_{2}$" x $2^{1}/_{4}$", unmarked, $125.00 – 150.00 set.

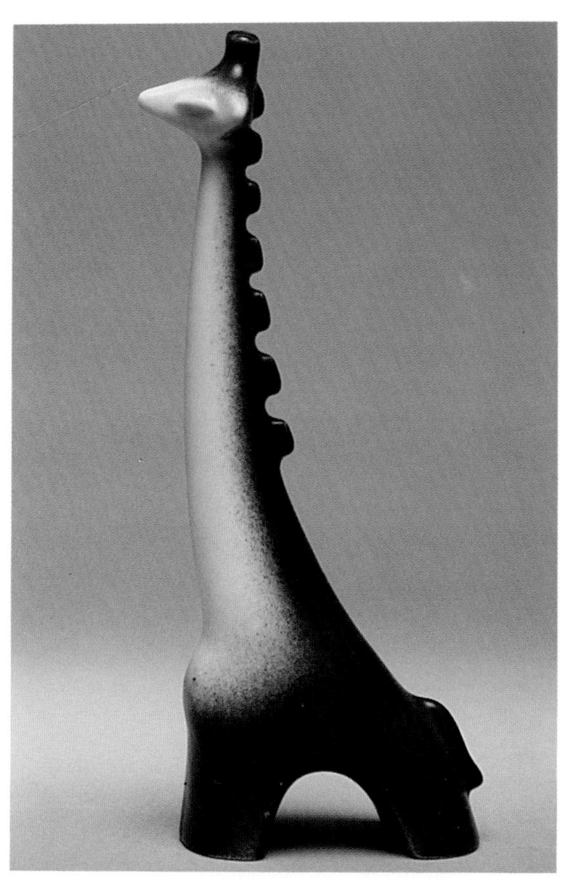

10" x 4" giraffe, "HOWARD PIERCE" black ink stamp, $75.00 – 85.00.

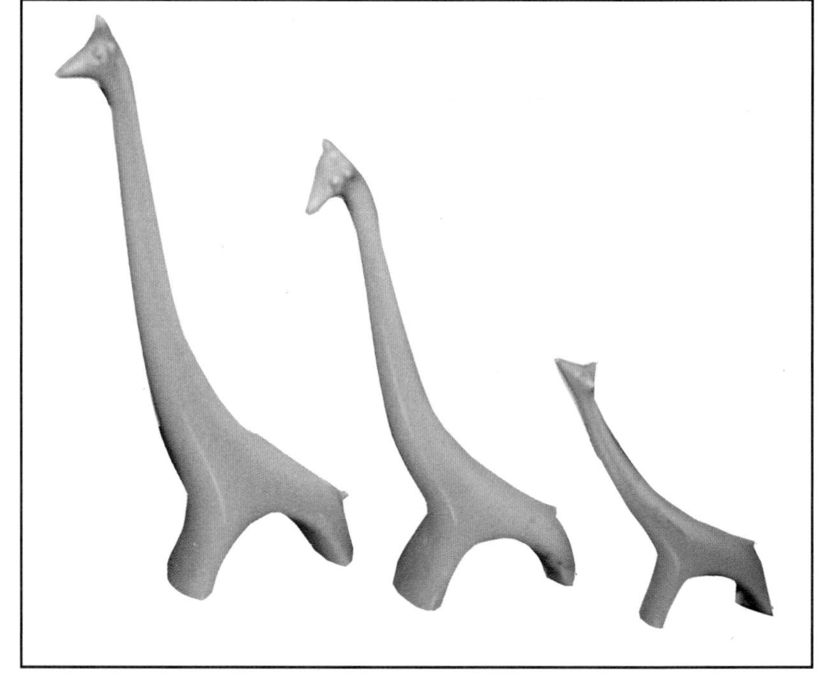

Rare delicate group of three 8", 6", and 2" giraffes, made for family, $300.00+. (Pierce Family Collection)

9" bison, unmarked, $150.00 – 175.00.
(Pierce Family Collection)

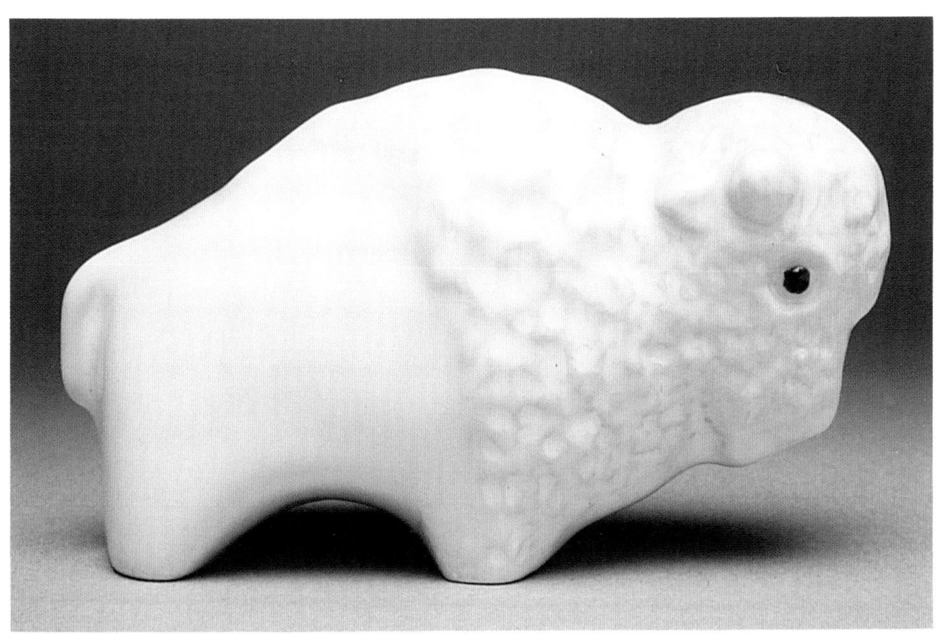

White high gloss bison, $2^{1}/_{2}$" x $3^{1}/_{3}$", black ink stamp "PIERCE," $50.00 – 75.00.

Mother and bear cub, cub 2¾" x 2", unmarked; mother 3" x 6½", "HOWARD PIERCE" black ink stamp, $50.00 – 75.00 set.

Cub and mother bear, standing on hind legs, 3¼" x 3¼" and 7" x 3¾", black ink stamp "HOWARD PIERCE," $100.00 – 125.00 set; high gloss black, gray, and white 4½" x 3¼" bear, black ink stamp "HOWARD PIERCE PORCELAIN," $75.00 – 100.00; shaggy 5" x 5½" mother and 3¼" x 3" cub, black ink stamp "HOWARD PIERCE," $100.00 – 125.00 set. (Ron and Juvelyn Nickel Collection)

Textured glaze bear cub, 3¼" x 5¼", "HOWARD PIERCE" black ink stamp, $65.00 – 75.00.

High gloss browish green glaze bear cub, $4^{3}/_{4}$" x $5^{1}/_{4}$", "HOWARD PIERCE" black ink stamp, $35.00 – 50.00.

Pair of koala bears, each $4^{1}/_{4}$" x $4^{1}/_{2}$", high gloss mottled glaze, brown ink stamp "HOWARD PIERCE" and dated "1991," $65.00 – 85.00 each.

Two white high gloss polar bears, not a set, adult $4^{1}/_{2}$" x $8^{1}/_{2}$", $175.00 – 200.00, cub 3" x 7", $125.00 – 150.00, both marked with black ink stamp "HOWARD PIERCE." (Ron & Juvelyn Nickel Collection)

Blue glaze hippopotamus, $2^{1}/_{2}$" x $6^{1}/_{2}$", black ink stamp "HOWARD PIERCE," $125.00 – 150.00. (Ron and Juvelyn Nickel Collection)

Rare 2" x 12" tiger with hand-painted stripes, black ink stamp "HOWARD PIERCE," $300.00+. (Ron and Juvelyn Nickel Collection)

Rare black high gloss panther, 2" x 12", marked "HOWARD PIERCE" with brown ink stamp, $200.00+. This is the same mold as that used for the tiger, but a different color. This mold was also used to make a leopard.

Llamas, mother $8^{1}/_{2}$" x 6", and baby $5^{1}/_{2}$" x $3^{1}/_{2}$", both unmarked, $175.00 – 200.00 set. (Ron and Juvelyn Nickel Collection)

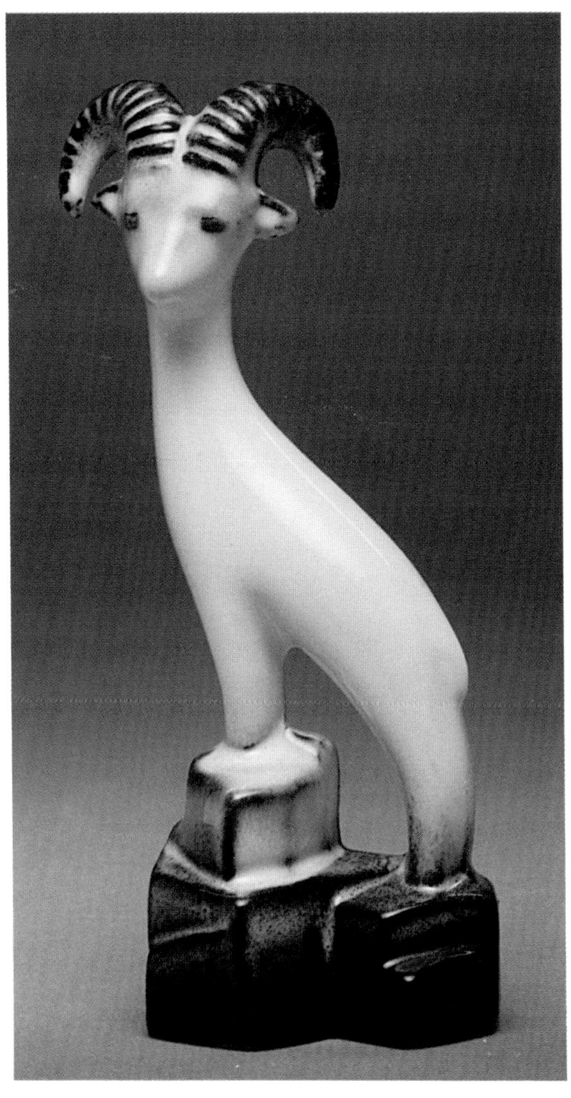

Mountain sheep ram, 7¼" x 3", black ink stamp "HOWARD PIERCE," $80.00 – 100.00. Mountain sheep were also known as bighorns because of the ram's massive spiraling headgear.

Rare 15" mountain goat, with bearded chin and backward-curving black horns, $350.00+. (Pierce Family Collection)

Monkey with matte gray flecked glaze with black highlights, 6¼" x 3", black ink stamp "HOWARD PIERCE," $75.00 – 85.00.

Three pairs of rabbits in brown, white, and gray high gloss glaze, all $3^{1}/_{4}$" x $3^{1}/_{2}$" and 4" x $2^{3}/_{4}$", marked with black ink stamp "HOWARD PIERCE" and handwritten in black ink "Pierce," $35.00 – 50.00 per set of two.

Pair of rabbits, $7^{1}/_{2}$" x 4" and 5" x 6", both marked "HOWARD PIERCE" with black ink stamp, $75.00 – 100.00 set.

Textured glaze raccoon 5" x $5^1/_4$", marked with black ink stamp "HOWARD PIERCE," \$60.00 – 75.00.

Pair of high gloss glaze raccoons, $3^1/_2$" x 9" lying on back, and sitting 6" x $6^1/_2$", both marked with black ink stamp "HOWARD PIERCE," \$125.00 – 150.00 pair. (Ron and Juvlyn Nickel Collection)

High gloss glaze raccoon, $3^1/_4$" x $8^1/_2$", brown ink stamp "HOWARD PIERCE" and hand signed "Pierce" with date "1991" in black ink, \$75.00 – 100.00.

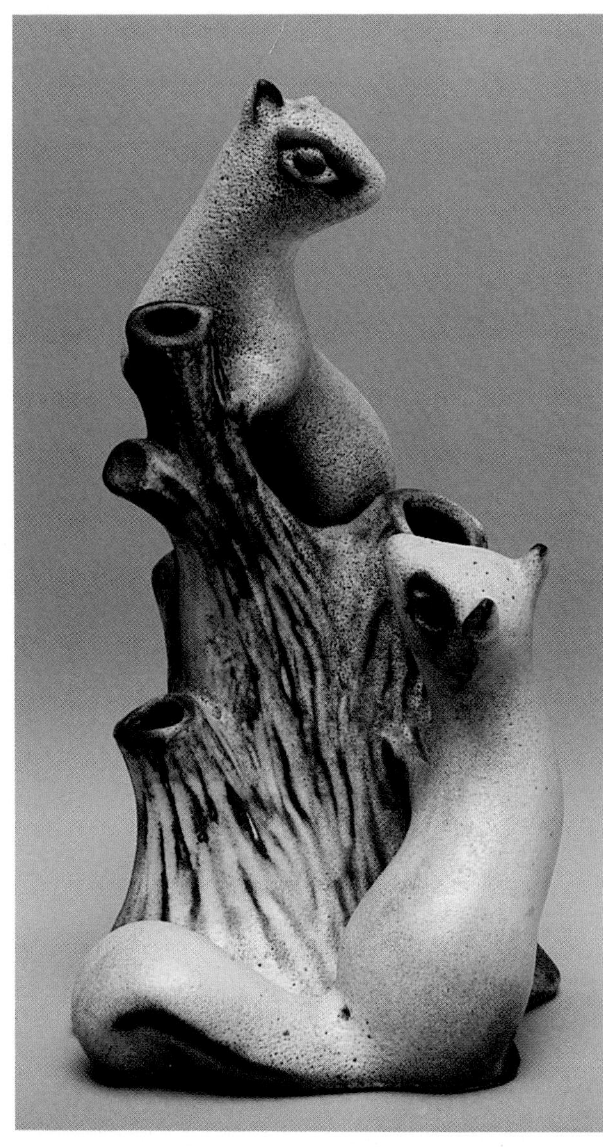

Two squirrels in tree, 11" x $6^{1}/_{2}$", black ink stamp "HOWARD PIERCE," $250.00 – 275.00.

White mottled high gloss glaze squirrel, $5^{1}/_{2}$" x $4^{3}/_{4}$", black ink stamp "HOWARD PIERCE," $60.00 – 75.00.

High gloss gray flecked glaze, four-stripes chipmunk, 2¼" x 7", unmarked, $25.00 – 35.00.

Pair of chipmunks, 3¾" x 1¾", black ink stamp "HOWARD PIERCE," and 1½" x 5¼", unmarked, $60.00 – 75.00 pair.

Two sets of chipmunks, brown mottled gloss glaze and white gloss glaze, standing on hind leg 4½" x 1¾", and on all fours 3½" x 6", all marked with brown ink stamp "HOWARD PIERCE" and handwritten "Pierce" in black ink, $60.00 – 75.00 per set.

Pair of beaver, 4$^{3}/_{4}$" x 4", black ink stamp "HOWARD PIERCE PORCELAIN" and 2$^{1}/_{2}$" x 5$^{1}/_{2}$", unmarked, $75.00 – 100.00 pair.

Pair of foxes, 5$^{1}/_{2}$" x 5" and 3" x 5$^{1}/_{2}$", both marked with black ink stamp "HOWARD PIERCE PORCELAIN," $75.00 – 100.00 pair. (Ron and Juvelyn Nickel Collection)

Porcupine, 4$^{1}/_{2}$" x 6", black ink stamp "HOWARD PIERCE," $75.00 – 100.00. (Ron and Juvelyn Nickel Collection)

5" x 6" skunk, black and white matte glaze, black ink stamp "HOWARD PIERCE," $80.00 – 100.00. (Ron and Juvelyn Nickel Collection)

Marine Life

$9^1/_2$" x $6^1/_2$" dolphin riding a wave, brown to black matte glaze with orange highlights, black ink stamp "HOWARD PIERCE", $175.00 – 200.00. (Pierce Family Collection)

Two dolphins riding waves, gray matte glaze, $4^1/_2$" x 7", "PIERCE" black ink stamp, $175.00 – 200.00; blue glaze, 5" x $7^3/_4$", "PIERCE" black ink stamp, $175.00 – 200.00. (Pierce Family Collection)

Pair of $3^1/_2$" x $4^1/_2$" textured white gloss glaze seal pups, "HOWARD PIERCE" black ink stamp and hand signed "Pierce" in black ink, paper sticker on one seal stated "Ruggles China & Gift House Disneyland California," $50.00 – 75.00 each.

Black high gloss seals, mother $5^1/_4$" x 6" and pup $2^1/_2$" x $3^1/_4$", black ink stamp "HOWARD PIERCE" on both, $100.00 – 125.00 set. (Ron and Juvelyn Nickel Collection)

Multicolor angel fish, $4^1/_2$" x 5" and 3" x 4", both marked with black ink stamp "HOWARD PIERCE," $125.00 – 150.00 set. (Ron and Juvelyn Nickel Collection)

Set of three fish riding waves, 6" x $4^1/_2$", 5" x $3^1/_2$", and 4" x $2^1/_2$", black ink stamp "HOWARD PIERCE" on each, $125.00 – 150.00 set. (Ron and Juvelyn Nickel Collection).

Birds

"Today, figures of birds are among the most sought after of all ceramic antiques. Entrancing lifelike or highly stylized figures often become coveted collectors' pieces as soon as they go on the market."[10]

Covey of three quail, baby 2½" x 3¼", unmarked, baby 4" x 3½", unmarked, mother 6" x 5¼", black ink stamp "Howard Pierce," $50.00 – 65.00 set. Speckles were spattered on these early quail with a toothbrush, which are considered the most commonly produced Pierce porcelain products.

Two quail on tree branch, 7" x 6½", black ink stamp "HOWARD PIERCE," $75.00 – 85.00; two families of three each, 4½" mother with 1½" and 1¼" babies. Both mothers marked with black ink handwritten "Pierce" and babies unmarked, $75.00 – 85.00 per set; set of two, 6¼" mother, 3¾" baby, both marked "HOWARD PIERCE" black ink stamp, $50.00 – 75.00 set. (Pierce Family Collection)

Two quail in tree, 9" x 3¼", black ink stamp "HOWARD PIERCE," $75.00 – 100.00.

Roadrunners on bases, male 9" x 12", and two females 6" x 9", black ink stamp "HOWARD PIERCE" mark on all, $75.00 – 100.00 male and $70.00 – 85.00 each female.

Roadrunner on large rock planter, 7" x 13½", black ink stamp "HOWARD PIERCE," $100.00 – 125.00. (Ron and Juvelyn Nickel Collection)

"Pigeons could just as easily be considered large doves since, except for their names, no clear-cut distinctions separate the two kinds of birds."[11]

Two sets of pigeons, 4½" x 7½" and 7¼" x 5¾", all marked with "HOWARD PIERCE" black ink stamp, $70.00 – 85.00 set.

Pair of blue high gloss glaze pigeons, $4^{1}/_{4}$" x $6^{1}/_{2}$" and 5" x 6", both marked with brown ink stamp "HOWARD PIERCE," $70.00 – 85.00 set.

High gloss white glaze pigeon, $5^{3}/_{4}$" x $5^{3}/_{4}$", black ink stamp "HOWARD PIERCE PORCELAINS," $65.00 – 75.00.

Black matte glaze pigeon, $7^{1}/_{4}$" x $5^{1}/_{2}$", black ink stamp "HOWARD PIERCE," $50.00 – 65.00.

$10\frac{1}{2}$" duck decoys, sold as singles, both marked with black ink stamp "HOWARD PIERCE," \$85.00 – 100.00 each. (Pierce Family Collection)

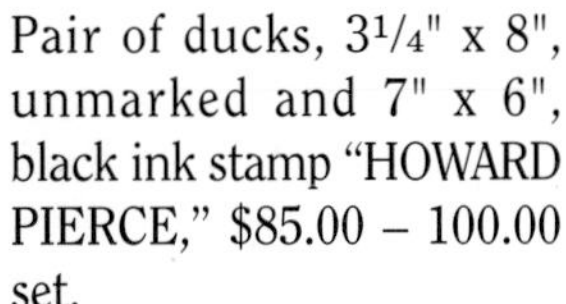

Pair of ducks, $3\frac{1}{4}$" x 8", unmarked and 7" x 6", black ink stamp "HOWARD PIERCE," \$85.00 – 100.00 set.

Baby ducks, 2½" x 3" and 2¾" x 3½", both unmarked, $25.00 – 35.00 set.

Pair of black high gloss glaze ducks, 4½" x 9", both marked with black ink stamp "HOWARD PIERCE" and handwritten "Pierce" in black ink, $75.00 – 85.00 each.

Hen 5¾" x 5", rooster 8¾" x 5", both marked "HOWARD PIERCE" with black ink stamp, $85.00 – 100.00 set.

Rooster 9¼" x 6", "©Howard Pierce" impressed into mold and "251P," $50.00 – 65.00.

Hen 5" x 4¼", unmarked; rooster 7" x 5½", "HOWARD PIERCE" black ink stamp, $85.00 – 100.00 set.

Pair of small white high gloss geese $5^{1}/_{4}$" x 3" and $2^{3}/_{4}$" x 5", both marked with black ink stamp "HOWARD PIERCE" and handwritten "Pierce" in black ink, $35.00 – 50.00 set.

Gray high gloss glaze goose, 7" x $6^{1}/_{4}$", black ink stamp "HOWARD PIERCE PORCELAIN," $25.00 – 35.00.

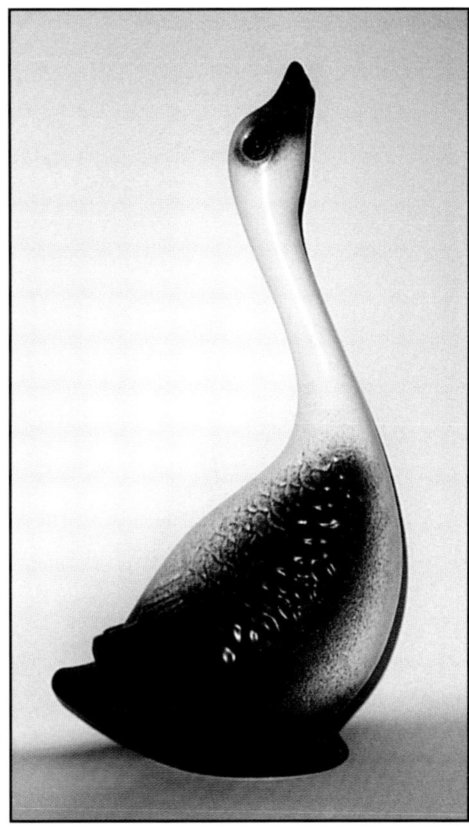

13" x 7" goose, black ink stamp "HOWARD PIERCE PORCELAIN," $100.00 – 125.00. (Ron and Juvelyn Nickel Collection)

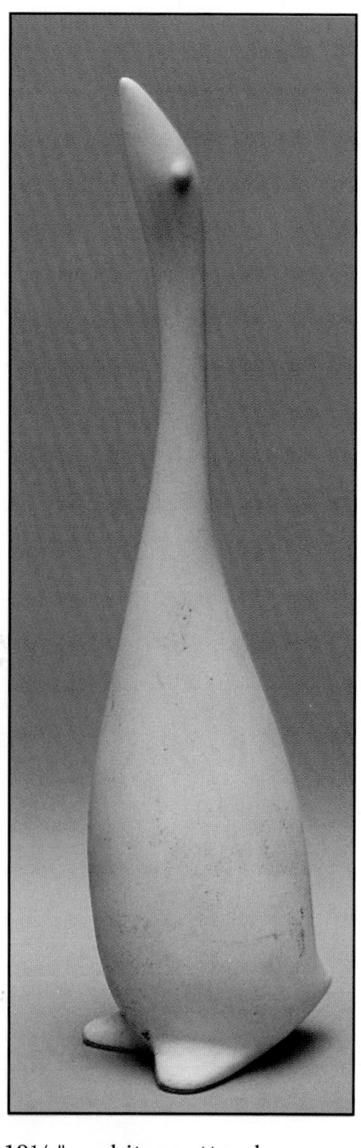

$13^1/_4$" , white matte glaze over red clay water bird, black ink stamp "HOWARD PIERCE," $60.00 – 70.00.

Gray to black matte glaze 12" x $3^1/_2$" water bird, black ink stamp "HOWARD PIERCE," $70.00 – 80.00; goose with sculptured wings, taking off for flight, $4^1/_2$" x 11", black ink stamp "HOWARD PIERCE PORCELAIN," $75.00 – 100.00. (Ron and Juvelyn Nickel Collection)

$7^1/_2$" x $4^1/_2$" pelican, black ink stamp "HOWARD PIERCE," $75.00 – 85.00.

Two pelicans, baby 4" x $2^1/_2$", unmarked, mother 7" x $3^1/_2$", marked "HOWARD PIERCE" with black ink stamp, $100.00 – 125.00 set; largest $8^1/_2$" x 6" pelican with pouch under bill, black ink stamp "HOWARD PIERCE," $100.00 – 125.00. (Ron and Juvelyn Nickel Collection)

White gloss glaze snow owls, 4" x $3\frac{3}{4}$", brown ink stamp "HOWARD PIERCE," with hand-signed black ink "Pierce," 3" x $2\frac{1}{2}$", black ink stamp "HOWARD PIERCE," with hand-signed black ink "Pierce," $25.00 – 35.00 each.

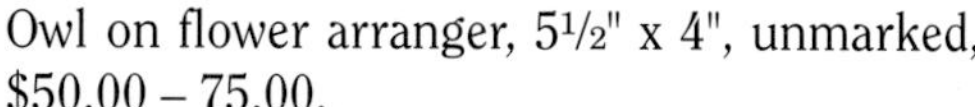

Owl on flower arranger, $5\frac{1}{2}$" x 4", unmarked, $50.00 – 75.00.

Green shaded to white matte glaze snow owls with black highlights, 3" x 2½" and 4" x 3½", both marked with "HOWARD PIERCE" black ink stamp, $25.00 – 35.00 each; horned owls, 5" x 3½", and 3" x 2½" black ink stamp "HOWARD PIERCE," $75.00 – 100.00 pair. (Ron and Juvelyn Nickel Collection)

Glossy mottled glaze vase with owl and foliage motif, 5" x 4", black ink stamp "HOWARD PIERCE PORCELAIN," $50.00 – 75.00.

Gloss white owl on planter, 6" x 6¾", black ink stamp "HOWARD PIERCE," $50.00 – 75.00.

Robin with orange breast, 4½" x 3½", black ink stamp "HOWARD PIERCE," $60.00 – 75.00.

High gloss gray bird with white breast, 2½" x 3½", unmarked, $25.00 – 35.00; high gloss gray bird on stump, 5" x 3½", black ink stamp "HOWARD PIERCE," $35.00 – 50.00; and high gloss brownish to gray glaze bird with white breast, 3¾" x 4¾", black ink stamp "HOWARD PIERCE," $35.00 – 50.00.

Colorful 6" x 4" red bird on black rock, black ink stamp "HOWARD PIERCE PORCELAIN," $75.00 – 85.00. (Ron and Juvelyn Nickel Collection)

Blue, black, and white high gloss glaze pair of parakeets, 4½" x 3½" and 5" x 2½", black ink stamp "HOWARD PIERCE PORCELAIN," $100.00 – 125.00 pair; yellow and black high gloss glaze goldfinches, singing 4" x 4½", eating 2½" x 3¾", black ink stamp "HOWARD PIERCE PORCELAIN," $100 – 125.00 pair. (Ron and Juvelyn Nickel Collection)

Rare dark gray 4" songbird with etched feathers, made for family, $250.00+. (Pierce Family Collection)

Brown and white high gloss glaze three birds on branch, 4" x 7", black ink stamp "HOWARD PIERCE," $75.00 – 100.00; two birds on stump, wings outstretched, 5½" x 5", "HOWARD PIERCE" black ink stamp, $75.00 – 85.00.

Three birds on branch in blue high gloss glaze, 4" x 7", brown ink stamp "HOWARD PIERCE," $75.00 – 100.00; two birds on stump, 5" x $2^{3}/_{4}$", "HOWARD PIERCE" black ink stamp, $65.00 – 75.00; one adult and two small birds on branch, $5^{1}/_{2}$" x 8", black ink stamp "HOWARD PIERCE," $75.00 – 100.00.

Pair of small birds, $1^{3}/_{4}$" x 3", unmarked, and $3^{1}/_{4}$" x $3^{3}/_{4}$", "PIERCE" black ink stamp, $25.00 – 35.00 each.

Large group with three birds in tree, 15½" x 6", black ink stamp "HOWARD PIERCE," $200.00 – 225.00. (Ron and Juvelyn Nickel Collection)

Penguins in black high gloss glaze with white breasts, large 4¾" x 1¾" and small 3½" x 1¼", all marked with "HOWARD PIERCE" black ink stamp, $45.00 – 60.00 each.

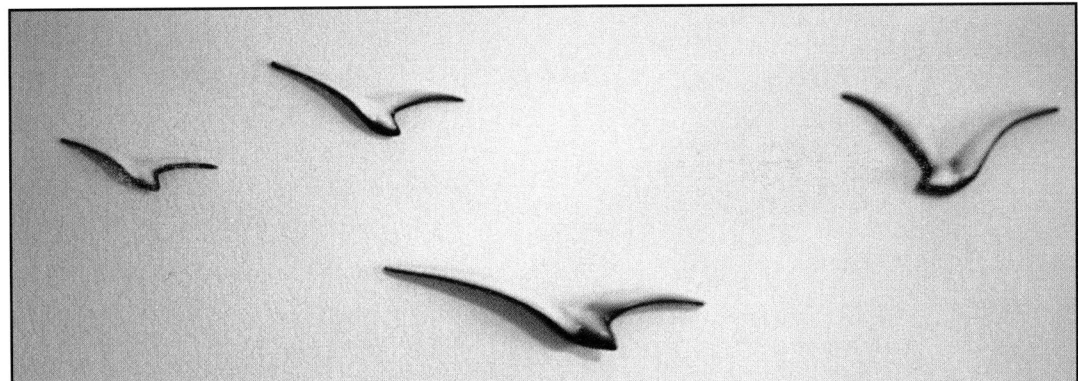

Rare seagull wall plaque, largest wing span 10" – 12" unmarked, $350.00+. (Pierce Family Collection)

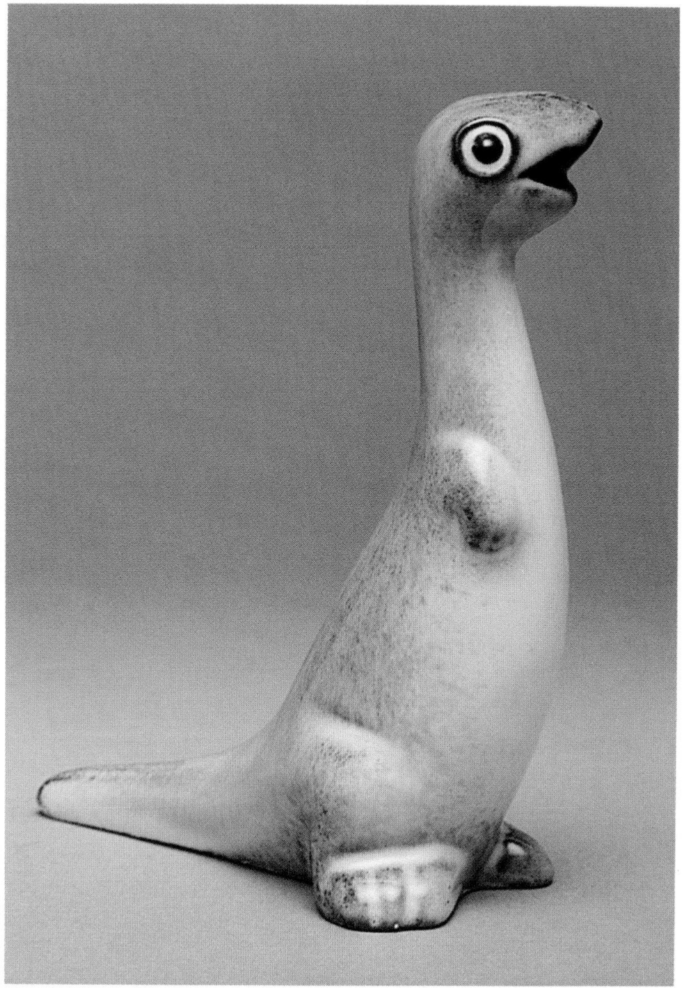

Dinosaur, $5^{1/2}$" x $4^{1/2}$", brown ink stamp "HOWARD PIERCE" and black ink hand dated "1991," $80.00 – 100.00.

Two unicorns, $5^{3/4}$" x $5^{1/2}$", both marked with "HOWARD PIERCE" brown ink stamp, $100.00 – 125.00 each.

Mouse, 2¼" x 3", "HOWARD PIERCE" black ink stamp and hand signed "Pierce" in black ink; two mice, both 2½" x 1¾", and marked "HOWARD PIERCE" with black ink stamp, $20.00 – 25.00 each. Mice were also made with rope and leather tails.

Warty-skinned toads, common in the Southwestern desert, spend most of their lives on dry land. All three toads, 3" x 3¾", with black ink stamp "HOWARD PIERCE" and hand signed "Pierce" in black ink, $50.00 – 65.00 each.

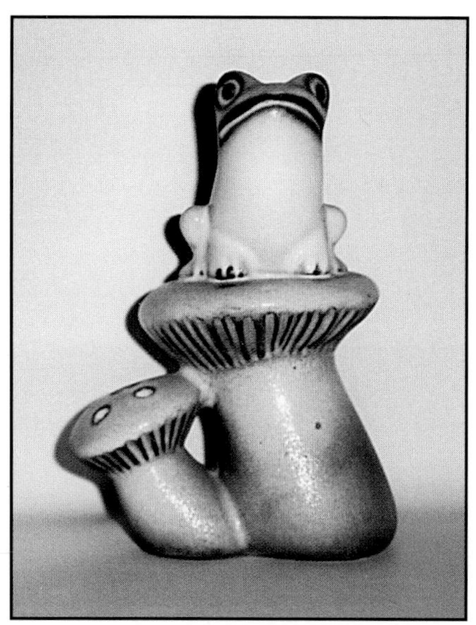

Frog with mushrooms, 7 1/2" x 5 1/2", black ink stamp "HOWARD PIERCE," $50.00 – 65.00. (Ron and Juvelyn Nickel Collection)

Rare white Hydrocal turtle, 1 1/4" x 3", black ink stamp "HOWARD PIERCE," $125.00+; all the following turtles are porcelain, rare white flower arranger 2 3/4 x 6 1/4", mark incised by hand "Pierce," $125.00+; brown with white 3 3/4" x 5", black ink stamp "HOWARD PIERCE" and handwritten in black ink "Howard Pierce 1987," $50.00 – 75.00; gold, 3 3/4" x 5", incised by hand "Pierce," $50.00 – 75.00; turtle on base, 6 1/4" x 4 1/4", black ink stamp "HOWARD PIERCE" and experimental glaze number/letter combination "60C" hand incised into clay, $50.00 – 75.00; two brown and white turtles, 1 3/4" x 4", both with brown ink stamp "HOWARD PIERCE" and "1993" in black ink by hand, $35.00 – 50.00 each; planter turtle, 4" x 6 1/2", black ink stamp "HOWARD PIERCE," $50.00 – 75.00. (Pierce Family Collection)

Rattle snake, 3" x 6", brown ink stamp "HOWARD PIERCE," $75.00 – 100.00.

$2^1/_2$" sugar and creamer, orange to yellow glaze, black ink stamp "HOWARD PIERCE PORCELAINS," $85.00 – 100.00 set; uncommon colorful hummingbird on flower arranger base, 6" x 4", handwritten in black ink "Pierce 1980," $150.00 – 175.00; purple and brown fish, $4^1/_2$" x $5^1/_2$", marked with black ink stamp "Howard Pierce," $50.00 – 75.00; rare blue interior flat turtle, $^1/_2$" x 5", black ink stamp "HOWARD PIERCE," $150.00+.The flat turtle was produced from a mold made over a plastic soap dish and not sold to the public. (Pierce Family Collection)

Howard working on figurine.

11" mother with baby, black ink stamp "PIERCE," \$75.00 – 85.00; 7½" child with doll and flower arranger behind, black ink stamp "HOWARD PIERCE," \$75.00 – 85.00; two children marked with black ink stamp "PIERCE" and handwritten black ink "Howard Pierce 1994," \$75.00 – 85.00; 10½" mother with child, marked with black ink stamp "PIERCE," \$75.00 – 85.00; 9¼" mother with child, black ink stamp "PIERCE," \$75.00 – 85.00. (Pierce Family Collection)

Girl holding open container beside two jugs, 9" x $3^{1}/_{2}$", black ink stamp "HOWARD PIERCE," $85.00 – 100.00.

Figure group of girl with dog, high gloss glaze, $4^{1}/_{2}$" x $3^{1}/_{4}$", black ink stamp "HOWARD PIERCE," $65.00 – 75.00.

$7^{1}/_{4}$" figurine of girl holding bird, greenish brown to blue matte glaze, black ink stamp "HOWARD PIERCE," $75.00 – 85.00.

Girl with long hair below shoulders holding bird, $7^{1}/_{4}$" x 3", black stamp "HOWARD PIERCE," $125.00 – 150.00. This long-haired version is less commonly found than the short-haired figurine in the preceeding photograph. (Bob and Clara Sweet Collection)

Rare 8" x 4" girl making music on mandolin, black ink stamp "HOWARD PIERCE," $150.00+. (Ron and Juvelyn Nickel Collection)

These "charming, whimsical figurines" were advertised as "designed and priced in pairs...a unique feature adding greatly to their decorative value and sales appeal."[12]

Native pair in brown/white matte glaze, 7¼" x 2½" and 7¾" x 3", black ink stamp "©HOWARD PIERCE," $150.00 – 175.00 pair.

Native female figurine in black/white matte glaze, 7¼" x 2½", black ink stamp "HOWARD PIERCE," $60.00 – 75.00.

Eskimos, sold only in brown/white color combination, $7^{1}/_{2}$" x $2^{1}/_{2}$" and $6^{1}/_{2}$" x $2^{1}/_{2}$", black ink stamp "HOWARD PIERCE," $150.00 – 175.00 pair.

Male ballet figurine 7" x $3^{1}/_{2}$", black and white combination, black ink stamp "HOWARD PIERCE," $75.00 – 85.00. The ballet pair was also made in brown/white. (Ron and Juvelyn Nickel Collection)

Hawaiians, 7" x 3" each, in black/white color, also made in brown/white, black ink stamp "HOWARD PIERCE," $150.00 – 175.00 pair. (Bob and Clara Sweet Collection)

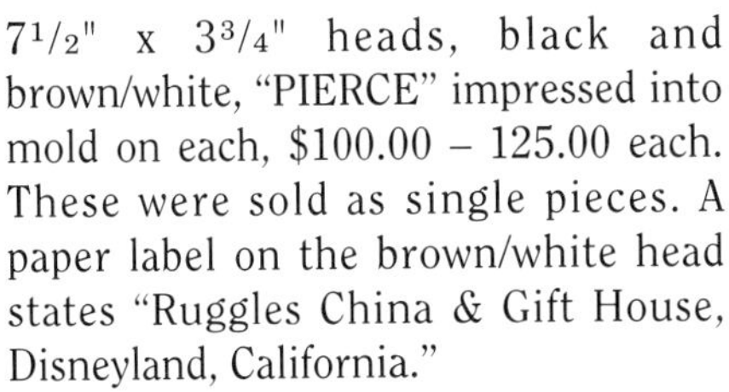

$7^{1}/_{2}$" x $3^{3}/_{4}$" heads, black and brown/white, "PIERCE" impressed into mold on each, $100.00 – 125.00 each. These were sold as single pieces. A paper label on the brown/white head states "Ruggles China & Gift House, Disneyland, California."

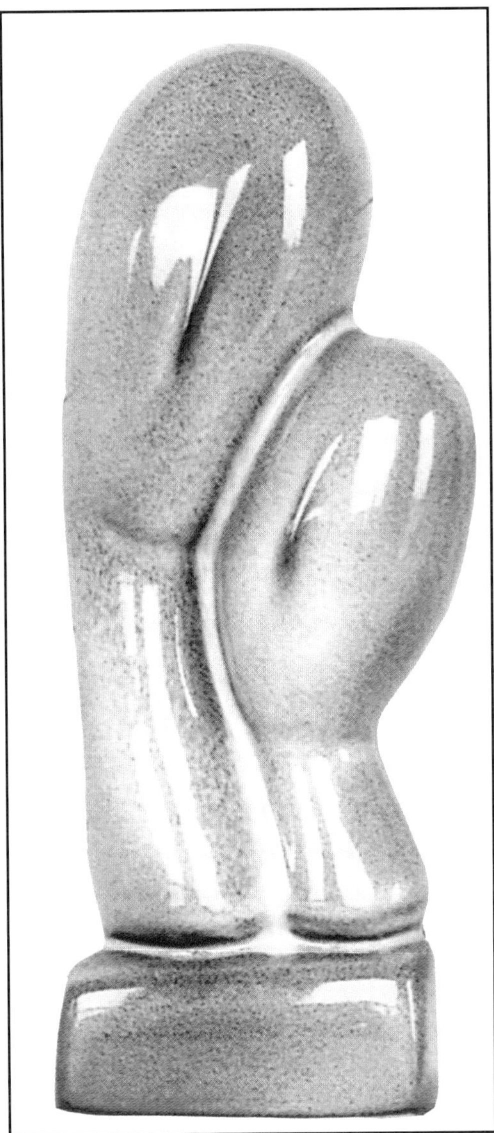

Rare 9" sculptural bust of two women's heads, $350.00+. (Bob and Clara Sweet Collection)

After Howard created a cup with images of female forms, the military wives told him, "You've made fun of us. Now make one with male figures."[13] Howard agreed and a male mug soon followed.

Group of rare items, female forms motif 4½" unmarked pencil holder, $150.00+ and unmarked 4" mug, $125.00+; male forms motif 4" mug, marked with initials incised by hand into mold "HP," $175.00+. (Pierce Family Collection)

Rare 7" vase with nudes motif, etched by hand, unmarked, $300.00+. (Pierce Family Collection)

Rare nude motifs etched by hand into 3" coffee cups, female and male, "HP" incised mark, $200.00+ each. (Pierce Family Collection)

A Christian himself, Howard created several figurines with religious themes.

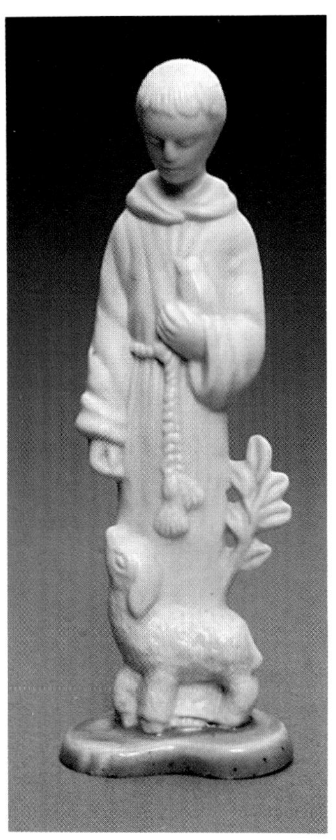

Rare white matte $5^{1}/_{2}$" St. Francis of Assisi, \$300.00+. (Pierce Family Collection)

St. Francis of Assisi with birds flower arranger, $11^{1}/_{2}$" x $6^{1}/_{2}$", greenish brown to blue matte glaze, unmarked, \$125.00 – 150.00. (Pierce Family Collection)

This set of black angels is rare. $4^{1}/_{2}$", 6", and 4", black ink stamp "HOWARD PIERCE" and "1987" in black ink by hand, \$250.00+. (Pierce Family Collection)

Three white high gloss angels. Singing 5¾" x 2", "HOWARD PIERCE" black ink stamp and dated "1991"; 4½" praying and 3¾" meditating, both marked with "HOWARD PIERCE" black ink stamp, $100.00 – 150.00 set.

Rare 8" angel illustating Pierce's creative use of materials as finished in part with brown shoe polish, $200.00+. (Pierce Family Collection)

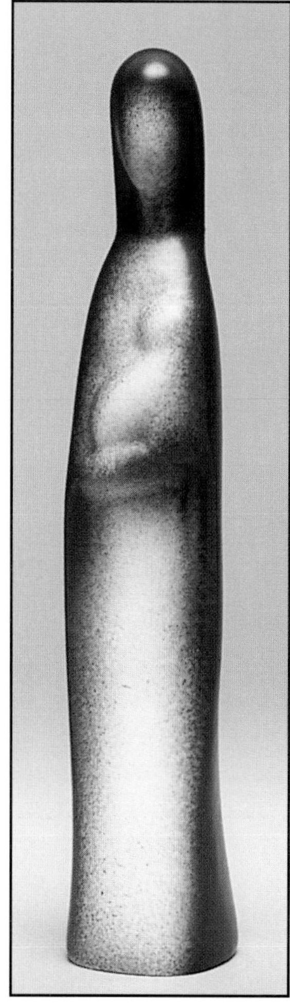

Madonna and Child, 13" x 2½", "HOWARD PIERCE" black ink stamp, $85.00 – 100.00.

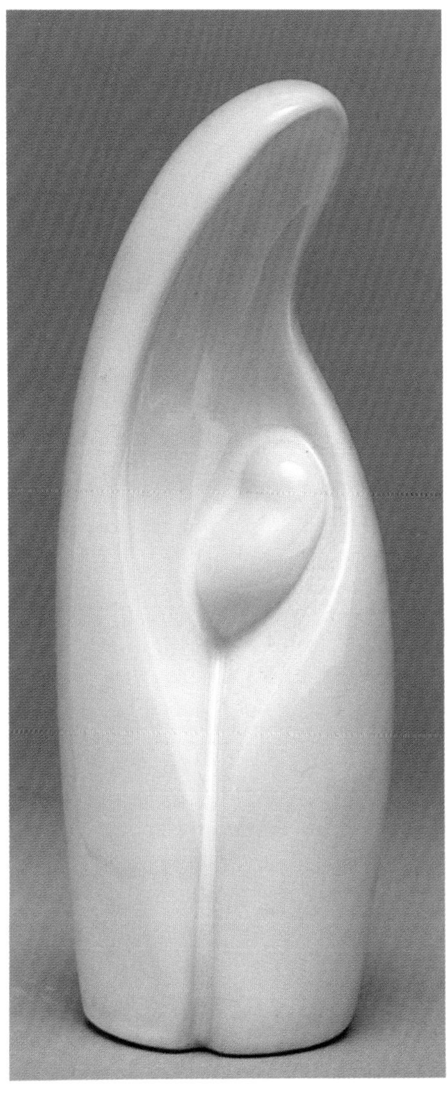

7$\frac{3}{4}$" Madonna and Child, white high gloss glaze, "HOWARD PIERCE" black ink stamp and handwritten "Pierce" in black ink, $85.00 – 100.00.

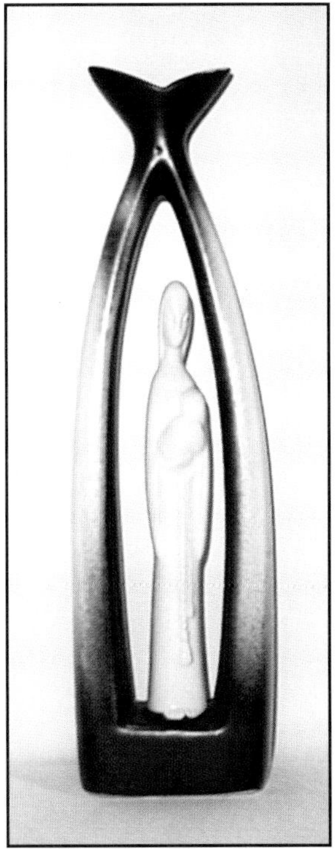

12" x 3$\frac{1}{4}$" arch with Madonna and Child inside, black ink stamp "HOWARD PIERCE," $150.00 – 175.00. (Ron and Juvelyn Nickel Collection)

White high gloss glaze Nativity set. Joseph 7$\frac{1}{4}$" x 1$\frac{1}{2}$", lamb 2" x 2$\frac{3}{4}$", Mary and baby Jesus 4$\frac{1}{4}$" x 1$\frac{1}{4}$", all marked with "HOWARD PIERCE" black ink stamp and "Pierce" handwritten in black ink, $100.00 – 125.00 set.

Brown/white high gloss glaze Nativity set. Joseph 7¼" x 1½", lamb 2" x 2¾", Mary and baby Jesus 4¼" x 1¼", all marked with "HOWARD PIERCE" black ink stamp and "Pierce" handwritten in black ink, $100.00 – 125.00 set.

Rare 9" and 7" monks, high gloss dark blue, tan, and white glaze, enjoy a good joke, $300.00+. (Pierce Family Collection)

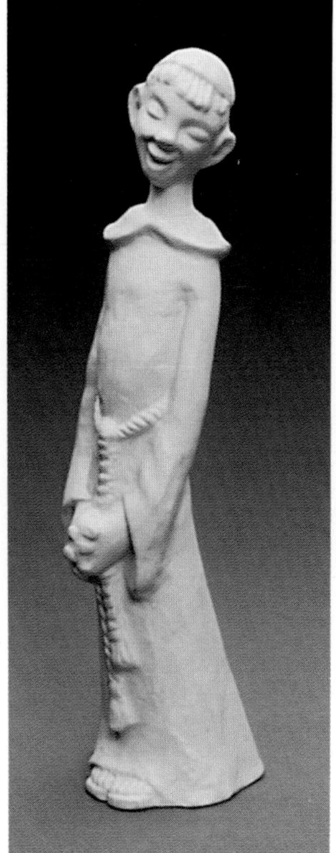

Rare 9" bisque monk, part of pair, like those pictured above, $200.00+. (Pierce Family Collection)

Functional Forms

In some of Howard Pierce's early ceramic work, the Manker influence may be observed. The striking use of two different colors inside and outside, spraying a contrasting color over a base color, sunburst effects, high gloss glaze, and fluted forms are examples.

Fluted metallic blue bowl with black highlights, 4½" x 7", black ink stamp "HOWARD PIERCE," $100.00 – 125.00. (Pierce Family Collection)

High glaze bowl, black background sprayed with contrasting blue, 4" x 6¼" marked with hand-incised "Pierce" and date "1991," $100.00 – 125.00.

Sunburst-effect bowl with aqua interior and black exterior, $2^{1}/_{2}$" x $7^{1}/_{2}$", marked with black ink stamp "HOWARD PIERCE PORCELAINS," $75.00 – 100.00.

$9^{1}/_{2}$" triangular bowl, aqua interior with glazed pooling effect and black exterior, black ink stamp "HOWARD PIERCE PORCELAIN," $75.00 – 100.00. (Pierce Family Collection)

Maroon bowl with gold interior, 4" x $8^{1}/_{2}$", unmarked, \$100.00 – 125.00. (Pierce Family Collection)

Rare large 12" circular dish with sea green mottled interior and brown exterior, "Pierce 1981" incised by hand, \$150.00+. (Pierce Family Collection)

BOWLS AND VASES

Colors: Lava (Brown), Sea Green

No.		Dozen Price
124-P	Low Round Bowl, 9" dia.	\$36.00
125-P	Low Fluted Bowl, 9½" dia.	36.00
126-P	Large Oval Bowl, 17½" x 9½"	90.00
127-P	Deep Round Bowl, 8½" x 4½"	48.00
128-P	Cylinder Vase, 7" hi. 4" dia.	30.00

Marketing flier.

Vases and bowls were advertised for utilitarian purposes, like flower arrangements as well as "purely for ornament. Lovely shapes that combine perfectly with the Howard Pierce Figurines."[14]

Flared top vase, 9" x 3½", brown ink stamp "©HOWARD PIERCE," $35.00 – 50.00.

Two textured vases, slanted top 9¾" x 3", straight top 9¾" x 3½", both marked with "HOWARD PIERCE" black ink stamp, $35.00 – 50.00.

Pair of low bowls, 3½" x 9", advertised as a deeper bowl for arrangement or planting, and 2" x 13", described as a graceful bowl, both marked with "Howard Pierce" impressed into mold, $35.00 – 50.00 each.

Gondola bowl, 5" x $9^1/_2$", black ink stamp "HOWARD PIERCE," $35.00 – 50.00.

$1^1/_2$" x 6" bowl, black ink stamp "HOWARD PIERCE," $25.00 – 35.00.

3½" vase with angular top, black ink stamp "HOWARD PIERCE," $35.00 – 50.00; volcanic ash outside, aqua glaze inside bowl, 1½" x 6", marked "Pierce" incised by hand, $65.00 – 75.00; rare 6" green to brown blended glaze vase on black base, black ink stamp "HOWARD PIERCE," $125.00+; 5½" vase with etched design, marked "Pierce" incised by hand, $75.00 – 100.00. (Pierce Family Collection)

Rectangular green planter, 5½" x 12", unmarked, $100.00 – 125.00. (Pierce Family Collection)

Individual ashtray "fits in the palm of your hand or rests securely on table. Safety notch holds cigarette firmly," advertising brochure notes.[15]

Ebony black and brown on white ashtrays, both 2" x 4", unmarked, $20.00 – 35.00 each.

Yellow and brown matte glaze 5" x 5" strawberry planter shape, incised "Pierce," $100.00 – 125.00. (Ron and Juvelyn Nickel Collection)

2¾" white candleholders, unmarked, $75.00 – 100.00 pair; 5½" white bowl, marked "HOWARD PIERCE PORCELAIN" with black ink stamp and "D-2" incised experimental mark, $70.00 – 100.00. (Pierce Family Collection)

Sculptural vase, 6½" x 6", incised mark "Pierce," $100.00 – 125.00. (Pierce Family Collection)

Rare 11" sculptural vase, unmarked, $200.00+. (Pierce Family Collection)

OTHER MEDIA

Howard also used other media besides clay, such as polyurethane, Hydrocal, concrete, pewter, bronze, aluminum, paper, and oils. Howard's experiments with fiberglass were generally unsuccessful, so this medium was used on only one mural. Items in the other media and outdoor sculpture sections, except the wall plaques, are not priced as they are one-of-a-kind or extremely rare and seldom appear on the market.

Polyurethane

Howard experimented with polyurethane in Joshua Tree for a few years. Polyurethane was mostly used for bird figurines, which were cast, trimmed, and then painted. Although this medium was successful in the creation of realistic images on naturalistic bases, Howard was soon forced to cease production because of an allergic reaction. The figurines, only sold locally, are easily recognizable, being hand painted, perched on different bases, and lighter in weight than the porcelain examples.

Hand-painted polyurethane birds on polyurethane bases, 4½" robin, "Pierce" incised on branch; 4" robin, unmarked; 6½" quail, "Pierce" incised on branch. (Pierce Family Collection)

Hand-painted polyurethane roadrunners on polyurethane bases, 5½" x 11½" and 9" x 8½", both "Pierce" incised on base side. (Pierce Family Collection)

Bluish color polyurethane birds on bases, 7¾" roadrunner, "Pierce" incised on base side; 4½" robin, unmarked; 5¼" goose, "1979" on bottom in red ink; 7" goose, "1979" on bottom in red ink. (Pierce Family Collection)

Polyurethane black horse on black base 9¾" x 9", unmarked. (Pierce Family Collection)

Polyurethane 7¼" gold goose on black base. (Pierce Family Collection)

Pewter

One-of-a-kind pewter $5\frac{3}{4}$" x $7\frac{1}{2}$" horse on black base, unmarked. (Pierce Family Collection)

This pewter horse, made by Howard for his mother before 1941, captures the movement and spirit of the animal. "Horses are amongst the most complex items to cast. Legs, tails, and ears must be cast individually and then rejoined to the main body."[1]

Aluminum

Howard made a few one-of-a-kind aluminum figures. "Sometimes when a mold was about to be retired and destroyed he would melt aluminum and carefully pour it in the mold. The water in the plaster would boil, causing wonderful cavities in the fast 'freezing' aluminum. This destroyed the mold. Probably only four to six pieces were ever made this way. He tried using lead, but the freeze patterns were not as pleasing as aluminum."[2]

Aluminum cats, 4" x $2\frac{1}{2}$" and 2" x $3\frac{3}{4}$", unmarked. (Pierce Family Collection)

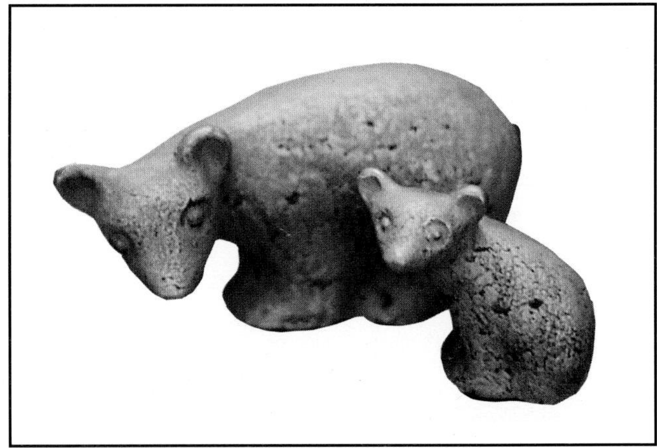

Aluminum bears, mother $4\frac{1}{2}$" x 7" and cub $3\frac{1}{4}$" x 4". (Pierce Family Collection)

Bronze

One-of-a-kind 25" x 25" fawn, cast in bronze. (Pierce Family Collection)

Incised mark on fawn.

In 1963, Howard designed a hardware series cast in bronze. Designs included quail and other flying birds and Native American motifs. Ellen stated that the company producing the switch plates did not follow agreements and production numbers are unknown.

Escutcheon switch plate, 10" x 10", with Northwest Native American motif. These pieces were evidently done in different materials. While this piece looks like aluminum or pewter, another family member owns one which looks like bronze. (Pierce Family Collection)

Gambel quail 8" x 5" switch plate in bronze. (Pierce Family Collection)

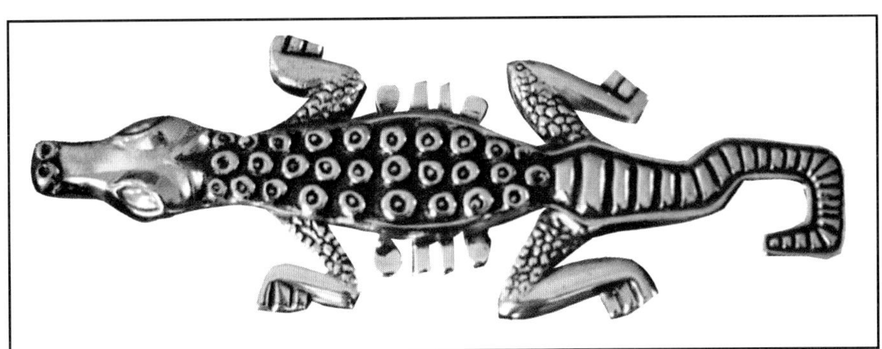

Bronze alligator door pull, 4¾" x 13½". (Pierce Family Collection)

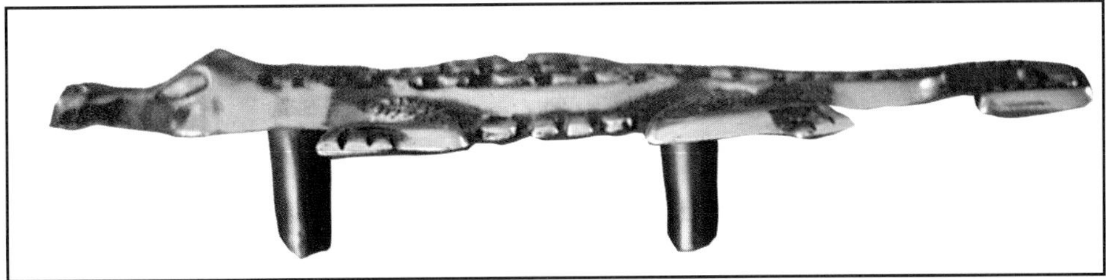

Hydrocal

Hydrocal is the tradename of a plaster-like sculpting material which may be purchased from a professional art supplier. When using Hydrocal, Howard first made the armature, the supporting framework. He then dipped pieces of polyester batting into Hydrocal and applied them to the armature to build the sculpture. The piece was then hand painted.

15" turkey, mostly painted Hydrocal, with metal legs. (Pierce Family Collection)

Hydrocal 11" x 7" quail, incised "Pierce" on side of base and bottom, dated "1988." (Ron and Juvelyn Nickel Collection)

8½" x 5½" Hydrocal squirrel, incised "Pierce" on side of base and handwritten in black ink "Howard Pierce" and "1989." (Ron and Juvelyn Nickel Collection)

Paper

Howard designed these cards which were then made by Howard and Ellen at a neighbor's house using a silk screen process. They were sent as Pierce Christmas cards.

Quail card. (Pierce Family Collection)

Roadrunner card. (Pierce Family Collection)

Painting

Howard Pierce disliked painting with oils and only completed two or three paintings. "He often wouldn't like what he had done and would paint over his work."[3]

Portrait of four-year-old grandson, Eric Self, painted by Howard Pierce in 1976. (Pierce Family Collection)

Concrete

With the use of concrete, Howard first fashioned the armature, adding the concrete later. Examples of these works also appear in other book sections.

Jerry and Howard applying concrete to the armature of the nine-foot "Howling Coyote" sculpture for the Fort Irwin Army Base, 1988.

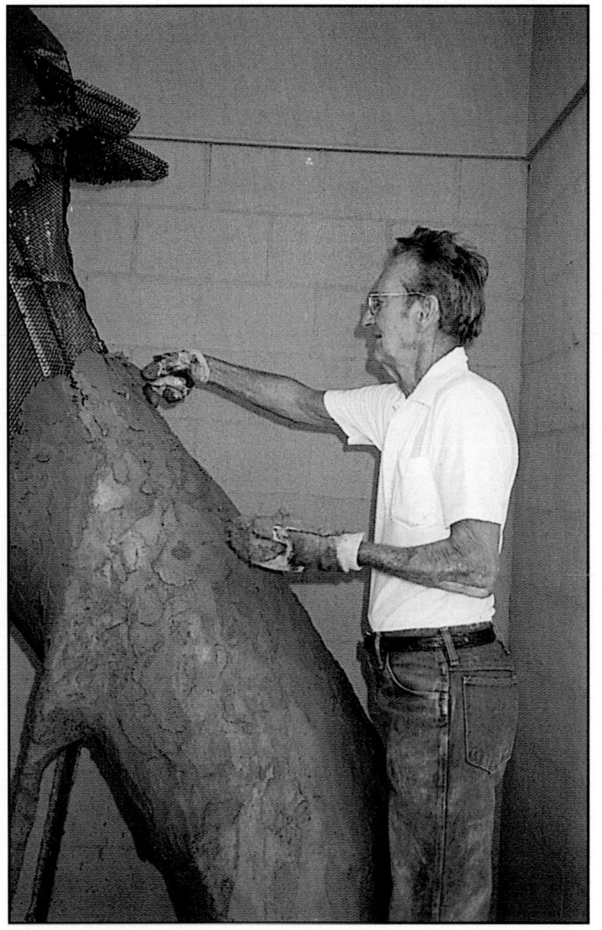

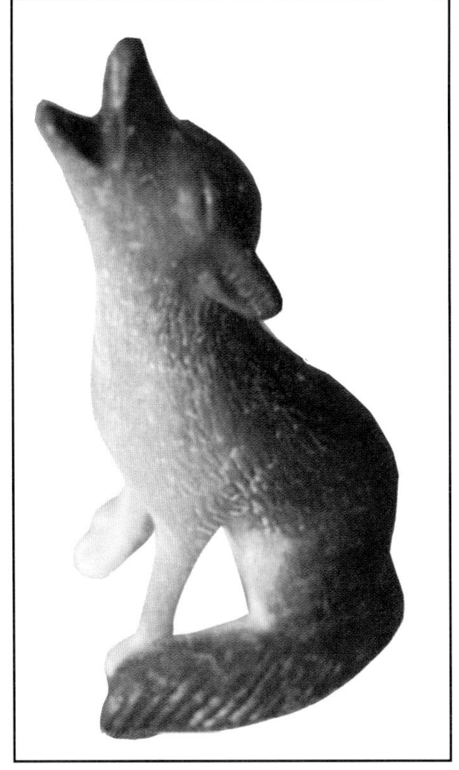

Smaller concrete coyote version, 15½" x 8". (Pierce Family Collection)

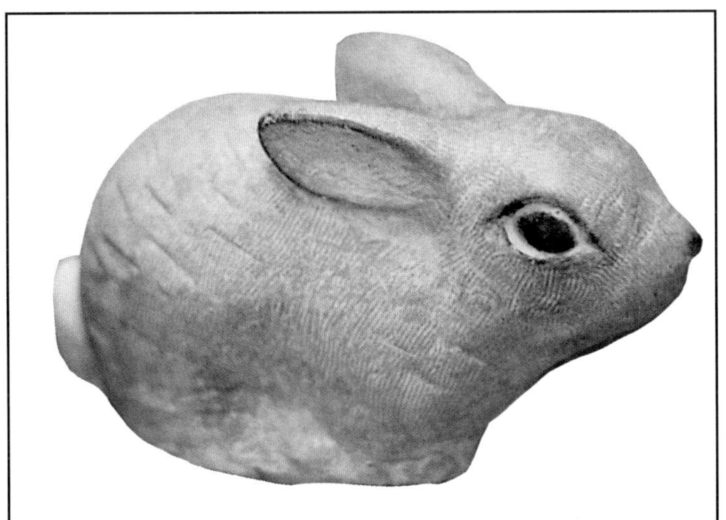

Concrete 5½" x 11" rabbit. (Pierce Family Collection)

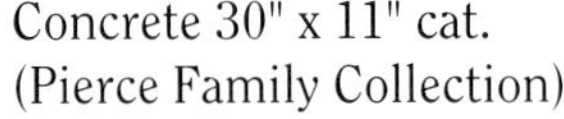

Concrete 30" x 11" cat. (Pierce Family Collection)

The tortoise, a land-dwelling turtle, has stout legs adapted for digging soil.

Concrete 10" desert tortoise. (Pierce Family Collection)

18" desert tortoise, natural shell from South America, concrete head, legs, and interior to support the shell. (Pierce Family Collection)

Concrete 6" x $7^1/_2$" walrus with pewter tusks. Howard left holes when making the piece and later inserted the pewter tusks and glued them in. (Pierce Family Collection)

Concrete 9" x 15" bison with pewter horns. (Pierce Family Collection)

One-of-a-kind mosaic made by setting pieces of glazed ceramics into concrete. (Pierce Family Collection)

Some of these wall plaques were made from plaster and concrete and others from polyurethane.

Howard Pierce with some of his castings, $200.00 – 500.00+.

Bluish white 5" x 12" casting of female motifs, handwritten in black ink "Howard Pierce," $200.00 – 250.00.

Songbirds plaque, pictured on side 12" x 4", unmarked, $200.00 – 250.00. (Pierce Family Collection)

Miscellaneous

Rare 26" x 17" raccoons plaque, \$500.00+. (Pierce Family Collection)

Early one-of-a kind sculpture of man playing piano, 4" x 4½", dated "1938" and incised "HOWARD PIERCE" on side of piece, unglazed and made from modeling clay, fired to a low temperature. The early date indicates that this piece was made either before or during the time Howard worked for William Manker Ceramics. (Ron and Juvelyn Nickel Collection)

Rare 17" x 12" Gambel quail plaque, \$500.00+. (Pierce Family Collection)

Bluish-black 6" unmarked monkey. Howard hand carved one using magnesium chloride. He then made a ceramic copy. The two were so identical family members could not tell them apart. (Pierce Family Collection)

Ceramic birds on wooden base, largest wingspan 12". (Pierce Family Collection)

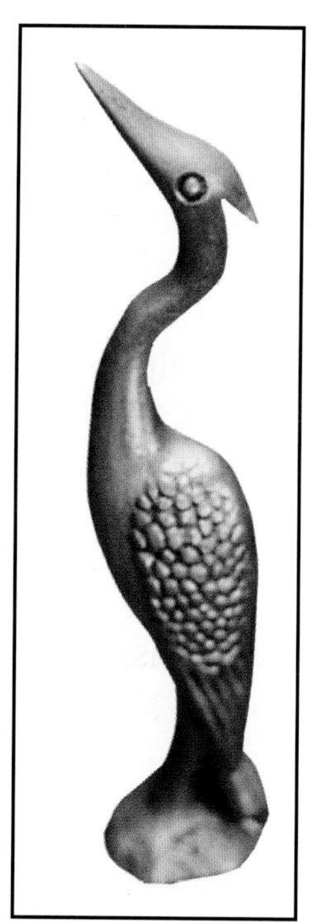

15" silver painted ceramic bird. (Pierce Family Collection)

Bronze painted ceramic fish, each 6" x 3", on Manzanita base. (Pierce Family Collection)

One-of-a-kind 27" x 53" mural of San Francisco. The plaster was cast in strips, cut, glued on a frame, painted with oil-base paint, and then antiqued. Howard later made one copy, using fiberglass. (Pierce Family Collection)

OUTDOOR SCULPTURE

Because "a garden is our link to the natural world, animals belong there."[1] Garden menageries historically charmed kings and pharaohs. Today, it may be difficult to maintain live animals in our gardens.

However, garden statuary provide artful substitutes. Animal sculpture has become very popular. Made to withstand wind and weather, sculptural animals are easy to care for and add life to our gardens.

Howard Pierce created several animal garden ornaments. Produced from concrete and finished with weather-resistant glazes, these critters may also be displayed inside. The animals were made for specific spots and not sold to the public.

Howard Pierce's larger pets, his cement menagerie, nestle into the rough terrain of their mountainside home. Inspired by his "twenty acres of rocks," Howard created these sculptured art works on the same scale. As visitors wound up the mountain to the Pierce scenic home studio, they would catch quick glimpses of Howard's giant friends.

It took four strapping young men to muscle the 500-pound, 8-foot high "Roadrunner Pete" to his place atop a huge boulder. Pete was then solidly bolted deep into his rocky perch overlooking Joshua Tree. Howard created this memorial sculpture after the death of his pet roadrunner, named Pete.

Concrete rabbit. (Pierce Family Collection)

"Roadrunner Pete." (Pierce Family Collection)

Concrete bison. (Pierce Family Collection)

Henry, the bighorn sheep, weighs in at 600 pounds. Originally named "Gertrude," Howard said her name "was changed when we found 'Gertrude' wouldn't have had spiraling horns."[2] Seven husky Marines placed "Big Horn Henry" in his rocky home.

"Other giant sculptures also blend into the terrain. A 200-pound rabbit, named "Pedro Conejo" (Spanish for rabbit) peers out of the brush. "Edgar," a 150-pound raven, named after the poet Edgar Allen Poe, scrutinizes the views from his lofty vantage point. The jet black raven, "among the deserts most conspicuous"[3] figures, looks similar to a crow but has a fan-shaped tail.

Although Howard enjoyed his impressive pets, he limited their number, finding just the right place for each. "I don't want the place to look like Disneyland,"[4] he stated. Each sculpture project took about six months to complete, as Howard made time from his pottery business. With chicken wire, wood, and pipe, he would construct a wire mesh frame and then build the shape from concrete. Different materials formed the final coat — boat resin on the roadrunner and brown cement on the sheep and rabbit.

"Big Horn Henry." (Pierce Family Collection)

Smaller prototype version of the raven, 11½" x 11", unmarked. (Pierce Family Collection)

"Pedro Conejo." (Pierce Family Collection)

MILITARY

Two nearby military installations were prominent in the Pierces' lives. The United States Marine Corps Air Ground Combat Center, Twentynine Palms, the world's largest Marine base occupying 932 square miles, is just a few miles away from Joshua Tree. Twentynine Palms, a town of 20,000, was named for 29 native filifera palms growing at its oasis. North of the marine base is Fort Irwin, a desert Army base.

Howard Pierce admired the military with their es spirit des corps attitude. He felt that they were "solid people."[1] In return, the military personnel and their families enjoyed the Pierces and became helpful friends.

Howard told of Marine families who liked to bring their guests to the mountain top studio. Many also purchased ceramics before moving to other locations. As a brigadier general, who served as commander general at the combat center, stated, "Much of your artwork is now spread all over the country and is rapidly becoming collector's items."[2] The Pierce personal papers include several letters of appreciation and thanks to Howard and Ellen for "outstanding support and assistance."[3] Through the Deputy Assistant Secretary of Defense, who visited the Pierce studio, a ceramic American eagle was presented to President Ronald Reagan in 1985. "I'm always delighted to be remembered by a fellow Californian, and the thoughtful concern that prompted you to share your work with me is truly appreciated,"[4] his letter reads.

In 1992, the officers' wives' club recognized Howard and Ellen as life-time members "for the numerous years of association both of you have shared with the Marine and Navy families stationed at the Marine Corps Air Ground Combat Center."[5] Howard and Ellen had also been honored by the Enlisted Officers and civilians' wives' club of Fort Irwin in 1989.

Howard and Ellen Pierce presented "Eagle," a twelve-foot replica of a bald eagle to the Marine Corps Combat Center in 1985 in appreciation for the good things that Marines do for the country. "I was never in the service," Pierce said, "but we sure appreciate everything servicemen do."[6]

Brigadier General William R. Etnyre, Commanding General of the combat center and the 7th Marines Amphibious Brigade unveiled and accepted the gift, personally thanking Howard Pierce on Armed Forces Day Open House. Several hundred Marines and guests attended the ceremonies.

Family presentation of "Eagle." Janet, Howard, Ellen, and Jerry.

Brigadier General William R. Etnyre and Howard Pierce.

Howard built the statue from colored concrete over a plywood armature in his spare time. The mounted bird weighed approximately 2,000 pounds.

Years later, a staff sergeant researched the history of the "concrete bird sentinel standing guard over the general's parade field."[7] He stated in the base newspaper, "I am glad he took the time to honor Marines here for their contributions. This statue provides a constant reminder"[8] of these contributions.

Postcard of "Eagle."

As our national symbol, the American bald eagle was an appropriate selection for the Marine base. The eagle became the triumphant central figure of the Great Seal, official insignia of our country, after six years of debate on June 20, 1782. Benjamin Franklin wanted the turkey as national bird but the eagle supporters won. "The new nation needed a symbol to represent its bold, free spirit to its own people and the world. The eagle, an important ancient symbol of Egyptian, Greek, and Roman conquerors, was an excellent choice. Eagle-like qualities of courage, loyalty, and freedom had brought the colonists to this land. Now, battle-weary, they needed an uplifting symbol to signify strength, majesty, and pride."[9]

Living almost exclusively in North America, the bald eagle is truly an American bird. "Bald" refers to the bird's white head with close-fitting feathers which create a bald appearance at a distance.

The United States military services use the American eagle motif extensively. The eagle, globe, and anchor of the United States Marines are well-known. Military items, like brass buttons, canteens, helmets, and belt plates display the eagle. Heroic servicemen are awarded the eagle on the Congressional Medal of Honor. The eagle also occupies a prominent position on the flag and seal of the Commander-in-Chief, the President of the United States.

"The bald eagle is no longer a mere bird of biological interest, but a symbol of the American ideals of freedom. With these words, the 1940 Bald Eagle Act of the United States Congress, protecting our national bird, expresses American sentiment for the eagle."[10]

9¾" artist's models of "Eagle" and "Roadrunners on a Base." (Pierce Family Collection)

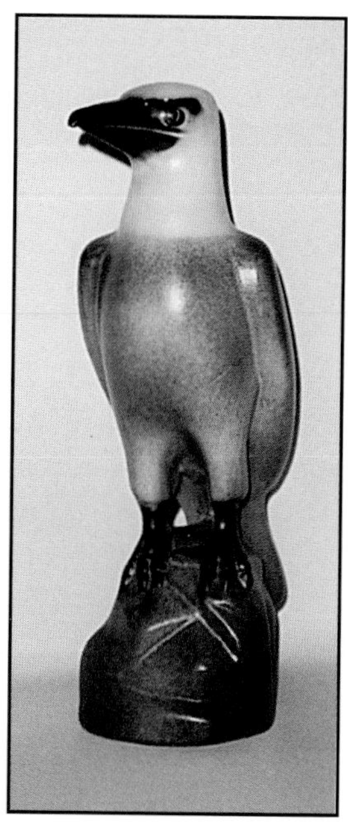

9½" x 4" porcelain version of eagle, black ink stamp "HOWARD PIERCE," $125.00 – 150.00. (Ron and Juvelyn Nickel Collection)

The 9' "Howling Coyote," the Pierce's only commissioned sculpture, made for the Fort Irwin Army Base, has proudly stood guard at the Visitors' Center entrance since its dedication in 1989. As a fitting mascot, the coyote statue "has become an instantaneous treasure of the post. Most of all, the Irwin mascot represents the hard working, caring, and wonderful folks who live, work, and fight on this ground to protect what the coyote lives to protect — its freedom."[11]

Recently, a Howard Pierce exhibit was featured at Twentynine Palms. As the local newspaper noted, "Pierce porcelains became favorite souvenir gifts presented to Marines and their families when they left their desert assignments to return to their homes in other parts of the country. The museum exhibit will enable them to recapture the enchantment of these unique art pieces now valued by collectors."[12]

Artist's model of "Howling Coyote," 10½" x 5". Porcelain version appears on page 36. These small versions were sold at the Fort Irwin base gift shop. (Pierce Family Collection)

Although Howard and Ellen Pierce kept a low profile, rarely participating in public events, "Most Morongo Basin residents have seen the Pierce statues which are placed in some of the most prominent places in the Hi-Desert community."[1] All these art works were donated to the community. Asked about their market value, Howard responded that he had no idea as none were ever sold. He estimated the raw materials for each statue around $400.00 to $500.00. "It's sort of a hobby. I just donate it to people I think can use it."[2] Ellen added that they target "important parts of our community."[3]

Restoring "Myrtle the Turtle," symbolic mascot of the community, to good health was the first major community project for the Pierces. Having "suffered from old age and exposure to the elements the past few years, only major surgery would cure her collective ills."[4] Howard and Ellen completely rebuilt the giant turtle shell from the frame up. Referring to a small model they first made to scale, the Pierces used reinforced cement to form a solid shape resistant to breaks and cracks. Observing a live desert tortoise, they then sculpted the details of Myrtle's huge, authentic shell. Painting with fiberglass plastic assured that the shell would hold its color and not fade.

Myrtle is now the rejuvenated official symbol of the community and the annual Joshua Tree Turtle races. As the parade turtle, Myrtle represents the area and its races on floats, escorting the queen and princesses. When not appearing in parades, Myrtle greets visitors at the edge of Joshua Tree.

"Myrtle the Turtle."

Donations to the Hi-Desert Medical Center provided new identity for the community hospital. "Family Group," designed by Pierce to represent the family orientation of the center, springs dramatically into the sky. The ten-foot tall, 800-pound concrete sculpture has become the official symbol of the hospital. A 12-inch ceramic version of the modern family image was also modeled for sale in the center gift shop. Howard made smaller porcelain versions of most of his concrete sculptures.

Medical Center sculpture.

Artist's 24" model of "Family Group." (Pierce Family Collection)

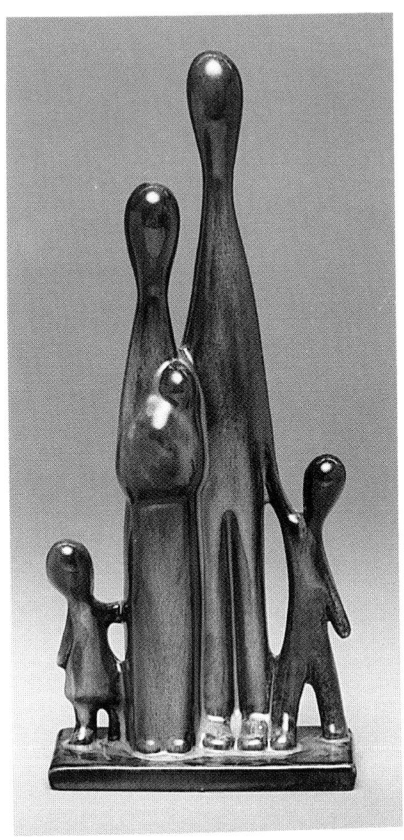

Porcelain version of "Family Group," 11 1/4" x 4 3/4", blue high gloss glaze, incised into mold "Pierce," $175.00 – 225.00.

Contributing to the world of local children, a Pierce four-foot reading girl sculpture welcomes children to the Yucca Valley Library.

Library sculpture.

Porcelain versions of "Reading Girl," 6 1/2" x 2 3/4" one in blue high gloss glaze and other in grayish brown high gloss glaze, both marked with "HOWARD PIERCE" black ink stamp, $75.00 – 85.00 each.

Two other Pierce concrete works were created for the Hi-Desert Medical Center. In "Jumping Dolphin," Pierce's cement dolphins decorate the hospital auxiliary building. "Memorial" adorns the hospital grounds.

Howard with "Memorial" sculture, December 1985.

Howard surprised the Friendly Hills School in Joshua Hall by calling to tell them he had a gift for "his neighborhood" school. "He constructed a beautiful hawk that we proudly placed by our flagpole. Shortly afterward, our hawk was stolen and again he surprised us with not one, but two beautiful hawks. He asked us to put one inside the building so the students would be able to enjoy it," stated the elementary school's principal Pat June.[5]

Howard and the hawk.

The Mountain View Cemetery, Joshua Tree, received a Pierce Gambel quail sculpture.

Spring 1987 photograph of Howard and cemetery sculpture.

Although Howard also created a condor mascot for the Condor Elementary School in Twentynine Palms, his daughter, Janet, stated that at first he didn't want to make a condor as he thought it was an ugly bird. Then he decided to make the head different so it wouldn't be ugly.[6]

Condor.

Howard and Ellen Pierce were honored in 1994 by the Chaparral Artists for their long-time support and participation in projects. A plaque is displayed at the Hi-Desert Playhouse Guild.

The Howard Pierce studio was featured on several art studio tours, sponsored by the Chaparral Artists. Howard and Ellen greeted their guests who arrived by shuttle bus to watch demonstrations and buy ceramics.

A six-foot roadrunner statue was a gift from the family after Howard's death and now stands in front of the Joshua Tree Cultural Center, home of the Hi-Desert Players Guild and the Chaparral Artists Guild.

The Hi-Desert Nature Museum continues as a tribute to Howard Pierce porcelains. Dedicated to "nature from the world around you,"[7] the museum is located in Yucca Valley, a city of 30,000 named for an exotic desert plant. Yucca Valley is on the tourist-promoted alternate route from San Bernadino, California, to Arizona.

Outside the building stands "Owls" a statue Pierce designed and created especially for donation to the museum. Two great horned owls, a parent and a young one, perch on a tree limb of the 2,000 pound statue.

Hi-Desert Nature Museum.

Howard Pierce's rendition of the great horned owl, the largest nocturnal desert bird, emphasizes long wings and large wide eyes. These wings are necessary to lift its large, heavy body. Large eyes give excellent nocturnal vision for night hunting as a powerful bird of prey.

This bird has survived several million years of evolution, with fossil finds indicating primitive forms of these birds existing 36 million years ago. The great horned owl "has few, if any, equals in its ability to thrive in almost any environment,"[8] and plays a beneficial "role by filling its niche in the skies over the Hi-Desert."[9]

Two 4" owls, black ink stamp "PIERCE," $35.00 – 50.00 each; two 2¼" turkeys, black ink stamp "PIERCE," and handwritten in black ink "Pierce 93," $40.00 – 50.00 each; 1½" baby bird, unmarked, $20.00 – 35.00; miniature version of "Owls" statue, 13" x 6½", black ink stamp "HOWARD PIERCE," $100.00 – 120.00; lava glaze 3¼" dove, black ink stamp "PIERCE," $65.00 – 85.00; 5½" eagle, black ink stamp "PIERCE," $75.00 – 100.00; Linda's 3¾" wood duck, black ink stamp "HOWARD PIERCE" and "1988" in black ink by hand, $75.00 – 85.00. (Pierce Family Collection)

A permanent exhibit of Pierce porcelains is on display at the Hi-Desert Museum. For years, the museum sold Pierce porcelains at the gift counter, including a smaller version of the "Owls" statue.

Copper Mountain College, Joshua Tree's college of the desert, has been the grateful recipient of several donations by Howard and Ellen Pierce. The college's CMC logo, a 2,000-pound sign of concrete created and donated by Howard Pierce, has adorned the college entrance since 1986. Pierce said he took on the project because, "since this campus was constructed, there was no sign here at all. Many people coming here who are not familiar with this campus simply didn't know what this facility was up here."[10] A small porcelain version of the sign was used for school fund raising.

CMC logo.

As visitors arrive at the public community college, they are surveyed by the Pierce sculpture "Roadrunners on a Base." (Artist's model of Roadrunners on a Base," page 112). A smaller version was also made.

"Roadrunners on a Base."

Porcelain version of "Roadrunners on a Base," 9" x 4½", brown ink stamp "HOWARD PIERCE" and hand signed "Pierce" in black ink, $100.00 – 125.00.

"Dancing Children," three girls dancing arm-in-arm in a fountain, is a "meditational or inspirational spot where people can come to rest"[11] on the Copper Mountain campus.

Armature for "Dancing Children."

Taking shape.

"Dancing Children" complete.

Further evidence of the Pierces' long-standing support for the college was their 1985 sponsorship of a room dedicated to the advancement of art in Phase II in the construction of Copper Mountain College and the donation of their kiln in 1992.

The college expressed its gratitude for the Pierces' artistic skill and dedication to the campus. "The Pierces have been good friends of this college for many years, helping us in ways big and small. I wish we could find a way to express the immense appreciation we have for them."[12] "We're really fortunate they live in the same community."[13]

The sculptures and contributions Howard and Ellen Pierce gave to their community continue to serve as memorials to these two staunch supporters, as their work lives on throughout the communities.

Howard and Ellen Pierce with one of their favorite sculptures, "Lonesome George."

CONCLUSION

An artist who wanted to be remembered for his work, Howard Pierce's porcelains became his legacy. "It's not what I am, it's what I do that's important."[1]

At a time when most pottery production was mechanized and the result of collaboration between artists and technicians within a company structure, Howard Pierce functioned as a studio potter. "All aspects of production were carried out by one individual, with assistance only in manual tasks."[2] Such an "artist-potter" required skills "beyond the clinical competence of ceramics."[3] Pierce's porcelains became "a unique expression of the potter."[4]

With their distinctive style and superior quality, Pierce porcelains have become highly-sought collectibles. As Howard Pierce captured the essence of animals and birds, these figures strike responsive chords with collectors.

The imagery of Pierce porcelains "stirs our senses and evokes our emotions."[5] Because Pierce porcelains are "a celebration of the beauty found in the ordinary world,"[6] collectors relate to them. As Pierce creations convey feelings and meanings along with visual images, the collector responds by searching out references in his or her self. Pierce porcelains with their "appealing balance between realism and fantasy, between the natural world and the imaginary,"[7] also challenge the collector to reformulate his visions and explore worlds unknown.

APPENDIX

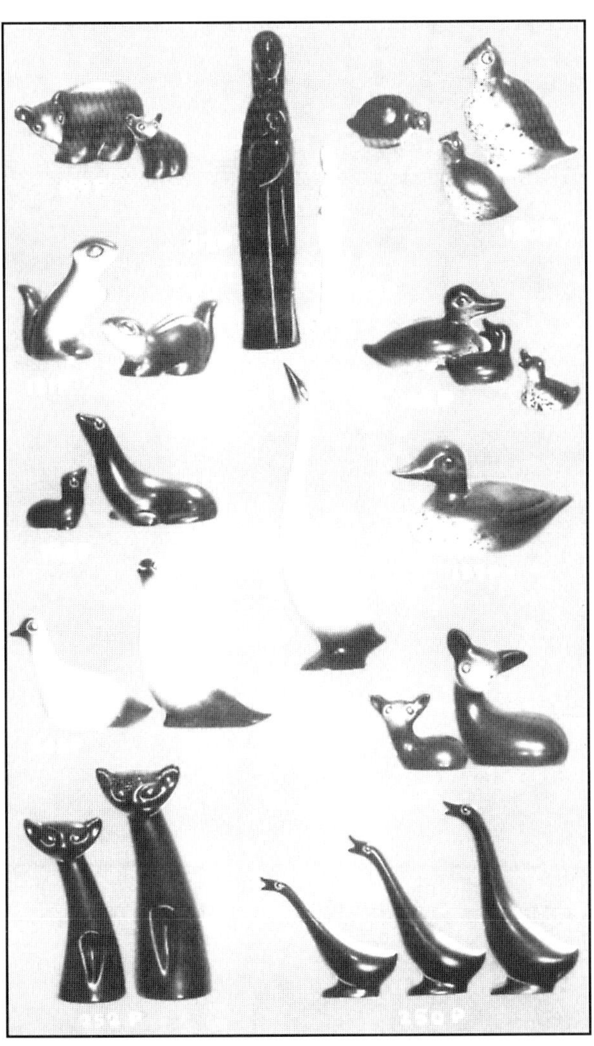

HOWARD PIERCE
Porcelain FIGURINES

Original designs, produced in porcelain by California Artist Howard Pierce. Sculptures of superb quality, modestly priced. Many of the numbers are designed and priced in sets of two or three...a unique feature that adds greatly to their decorative value.

Colors: Brown, Gloss Black, White.
(See description below for colors of individual items.)

No.	Colors Available	Dozen Price
112-P Madonna 7½"	Bl., Wh.	$9.00
212-P Madonna 13½"	Bl., Wh.	24.00
129-P Bear, Set of 2	Br.	15.00
130-P Quail, Set of 3	Br.	24.00
131-P Chipmunk, Set of 2	Br.	18.00
132-P Ducks, Set of 3	Br.	18.00
133-P Decoy Duck (Single pc.)	Br.	18.00
138-P Seal, Set of 2	Bl.	18.00
209-P Pigeon, Set of 2	Br., Wh.	24.00
210-P Water Bird (Single pc.)	Br., Bl., Wh.	24.00
211-P Fawn, Set of 2	Br.	24.00
250-P Geese, Set of 3	Br., Bl., Wh.	30.00
252-P Cat, Set of 2	Br., Bl., Wh.	30.00

Advertising Flier.

N. S. Gustin marketing brochure.

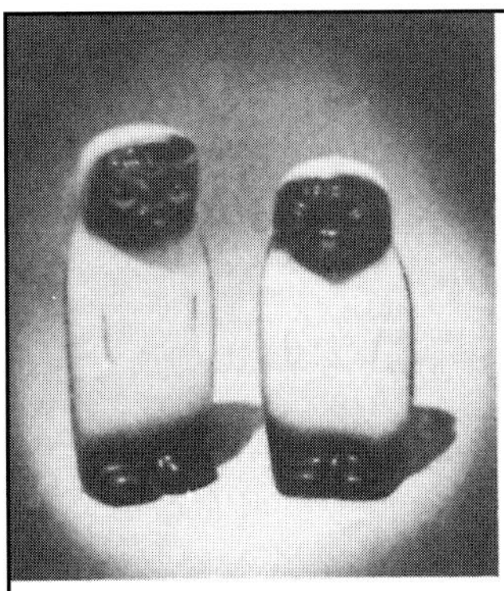

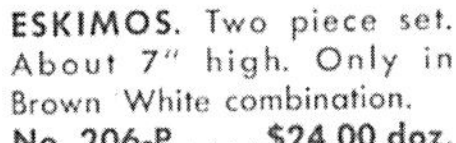

ESKIMOS. Two piece set. About 7" high. Only in Brown/White combination.
No. 206-P . . . . $24.00 doz.

NATIVE PAIR. Set of 2. About 7" high. Colors: Brown/White; Black/White.
No. 253-P . . . . $30.00 doz.

HAWAIIANS. Boy and girl. Tallest is 7" high. Colors: Brown/White; Black/White.
No. 256-P . . . . $30.00 doz.

the contemporary look in porcelain...

Charming, whimsical figurines . . . beautifully finished in satin-matte glazes by California artist Howard Pierce. Superb quality, fresh designs and very reasonable prices have made this a best selling line in gift departments everywhere.

Most of the numbers are designed and priced in pairs . . . a unique feature adding greatly to their decorative value and sales appeal.

Colors: Brown on White; Black on White; All Black. See description of individual number for colors available.

BALLET PAIR. Set of 2. Tallest about 7". Colors: Brown/White; Black/White.
No. 255-P . . . . $30.00 doz.

HEAD. A single piece. About 7½" high. Colors: Brown/White; All Black.
No. 254-P . . . . $30.00 doz.

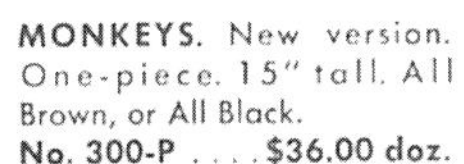

MONKEYS. New version. One-piece. 15" tall. All Brown, or All Black.
No. 300-P . . . . $36.00 doz.

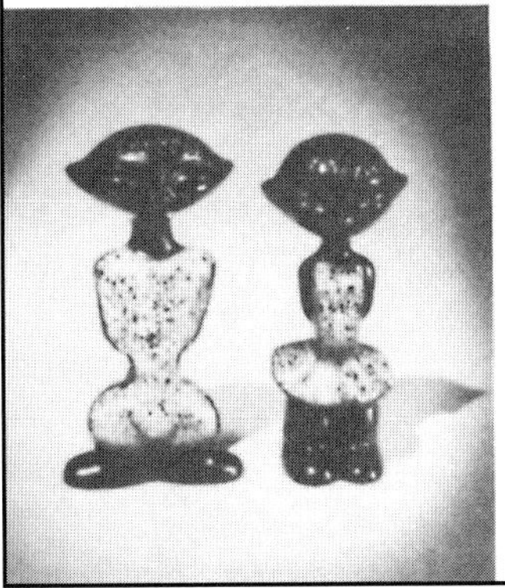

PELICAN. Single figurine about 8" high. Made only in Brown and White combination.
No. 128-P . . . . $15.00 doz.

BEAR WITH CUB. Set of 2. Large figure. 6" long. Brown/White; Black/White.
No. 129-P . . . . $12.00 doz.

QUAIL. Set of 3. Large figure. 5" high. Colors: Brown/White; Brown Speckled.
No. 130-P . . . . $18.00 doz.

FISH. Set of 3. Large is about 6" high. Colors: Brown or Black Speckled.
No. 203-P . . . . $24.00 doz.

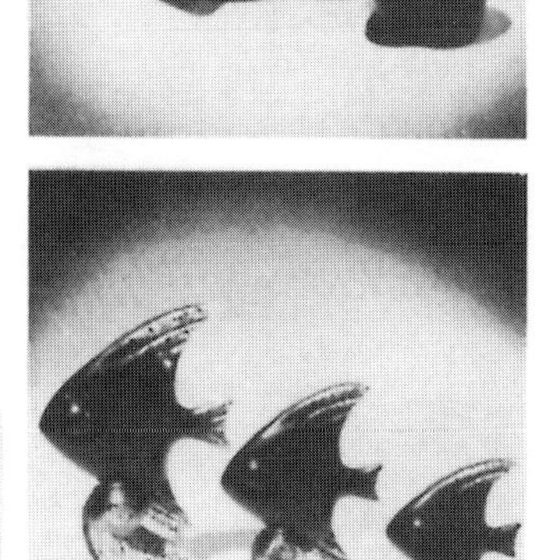

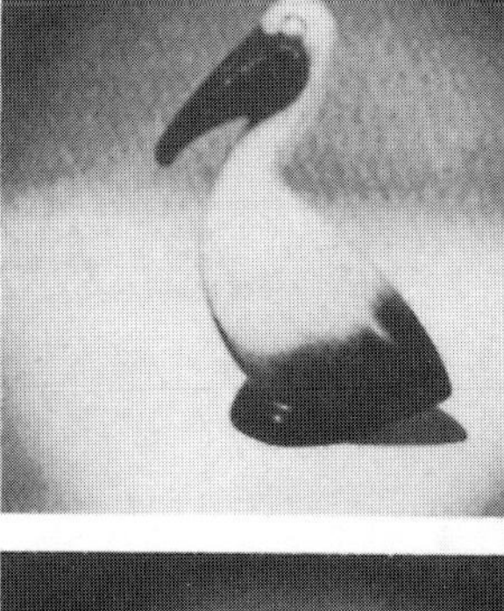

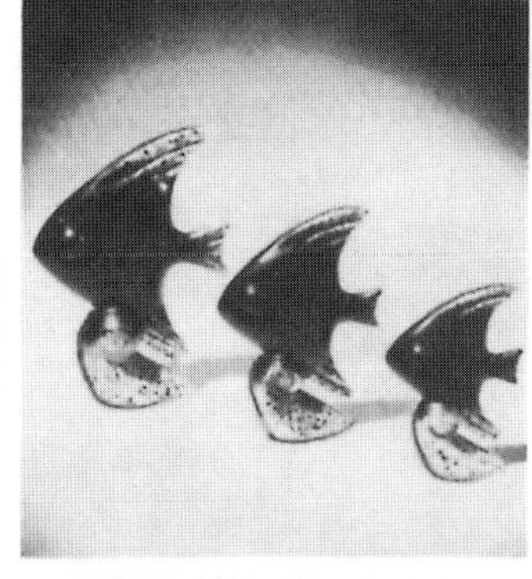

2 GEESE AND A GANDER. 3 piece set. About 8" high. Brown/White; All Black.
No. 250-P . . . . $30.00 doz.

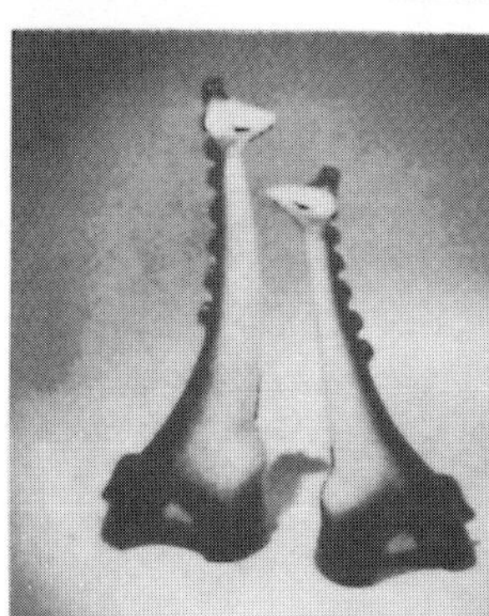

GIRAFFES. Set of 2. Tall figure about 10". Color: Brown/White only.
No. 204-P . . . . $24.00 doz.

DOGS. Set of 2. Large figure 7" high. Made in Brown/White only.
No. 205-P . . . . $24.00 doz.

CATS. Two piece set. Tallest about 10" high. Brown/White; All Black.
No. 252-P . . . . $30.00 doz.

ERMINE. Set of 2. Large figure about 9" high. This pair in Brown/White only.
No. 257-P . . . . $30.00 doz.

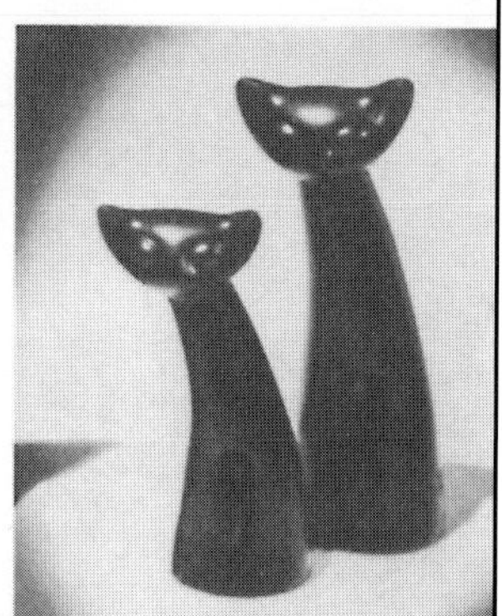

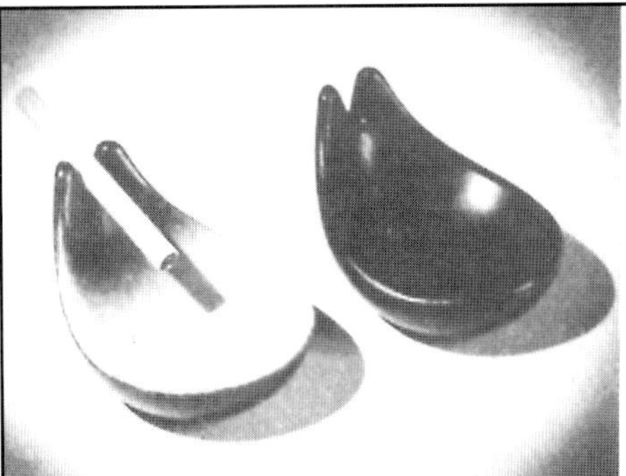

Handy! Individual ash tray fits in the palm of your hand, or rests securely on table. Safety notch holds cigarette firmly. Sell them singly, or in sets. Satin smooth porcelain in ebony black or brown on white. About 4" long.
No. 100-P . . . . $6.00 dozen

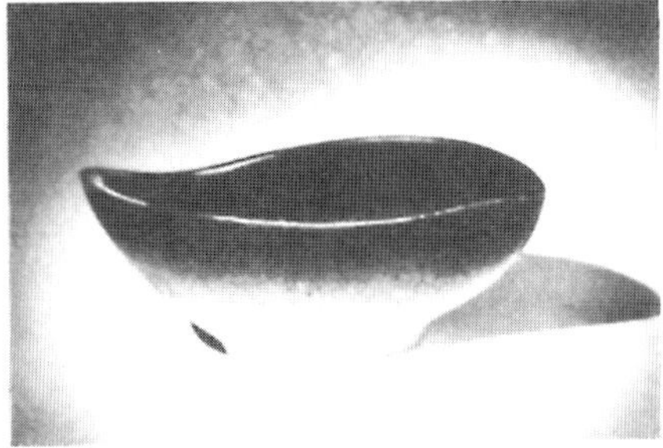

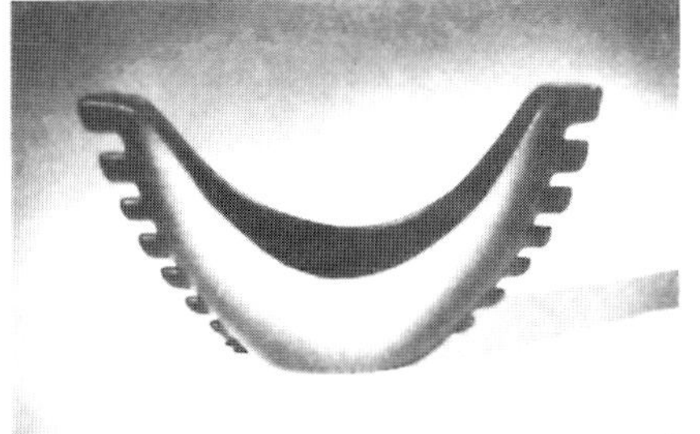

Bowls for flower arrangements, or purely for ornament. Lovely shapes that combine perfectly with the Howard Pierce Figurines. Three numbers as illustrated suggest many bowl-figurine combinations to increase sales and spark up displays. Bowl colors match figurines.

A smart, graceful bowl about 13" long. Two-tone colors: Brown on White, or Black on White.
No. 150-P . . . . $18.00 dozen

Deeper bowl 9" long for arrangement, or planting. Colors: Brown on White, or Black on White.
No. 151-P . . . . $18.00 dozen

Gondola Bowl. An unusual shape. About 9" across. Available in Brown on White color only.
No. 201-P . . . . . . $[illegible]4.00 dozen

All Prices F.O.B. Claremont, Calif.
Terms: 2% 10 days, net 30 days

N. S. GUSTIN COMPANY
712 SOUTH OLIVE ST. • LOS ANGELES 14, CALIF.

NEW YORK • 225 FIFTH AVENUE
CHICAGO • 1583 MERCH. MART

END NOTES

Introduction

1. Andersen, Moore, and Winter, 8.
2. Chipman, Introduction.
3. Pellecchia, E11.
4. "The British Virgin Islands," promotional brochure (New York: British Virgin Islands Tourist Board, 1994).
5. Lubbock, 175.
6. Doulton, 40.
7. Lubbock, 179.
8. McGuire, An Interview with the Artist.
9. Olson, 129.
10. Andersen, 8.
11. "contemporary porcelain: howard pierce design." N. S. Gustin Company marketing brochure.
12. Lubbock, 181.
13. Herr, 14.
14. "Puffed Tuffins," 12.
15. Ellen Pierce, interview. Information derived from several interviews in person, written correspondence, and telephone calls appears throughout the book.
16. Cornfield and Edwards, Introduction.
17. Lewis, 7.
18. Cornfield, Introduction.

History

1. Mireles, 7.
2. Howard Pierce, interview. Information derived from interviews in person contributed throughout the book.
3. Howard Pierce, interview.
4. Chipman, 56.
5. "Robinsons' Gift Accents 1941," Vogue, 1941.
6. Ellen Pierce, interview.
7. Howard Pierce, interview.
8. Ibid.
9. Mireles, 8.
10. Howard Pierce, interview.
11. Ellen Pierce, interview.
12. Mireles, 8.
13. Linda Pierce Picciotto, interview. Linda also contributed other factual and technical material to the book.
14. Piciotto, interview.
15. Ibid.
16. Ellen Pierce, interview.
17. Ibid.
18. Piciotto, correspondence.
19. Piciotto, interview.
20. Ibid.
21. Ellen Pierce, interview.
22. Howard Pierce, interview.
23. Ibid.
24. Mireles, 8.
25. Ibid.
26. "contemporary porcelain: howard pierce design." N. S. Gustin Company marketing brochure.
27. Lewis, 7.
28. *Mobil Travel Guide: California and the West*, 130.
29. *Off the Beaten Path*, 353.
30. Mireles, 7.
31. Ibid.
32. Ibid.
33. Ellen Pierce, interview.

34. Ibid.
35. Cornett, 9.
36. Welles, IX.
37. Blietz, A2.
38. Ellen Pierce, correspondence.
39. Picciotto, correspondence.
40. Blietz, A2.
41. Ellen Pierce, interview.
42. Howard Pierce, interview.
43. Piciotto, interview.
44. Ellen Pierce, interview.
45. Binns, 165.
46. Howard Pierce interview.
47. Ibid.
48 Jerry Pierce, interview.
49. Blietz, A3.
50 Howard Pierce, interview.

Porcelain Process

1. Howard Pierce, interview.
2. Binns, "Clay in the Potter's Hand," 164.
3. Binns, 162.
4. Binns, The Potter's Craft, 12.
5. Ellen Pierce, interview.
6. Picciotto, "HW Pierce Glazes and Clay: Notes From My Notebook," 1996.
7. Cox, 16.
8. Howard Pierce, interview.
9. Ibid.
10. Ibid.

Collecting

1. Blietz, A1.
2. Piciotto, interview.
3. Howard Pierce, interview.
4. Nelson, 84.
5. Trapp, 161.
6. Ellen Pierce, interview.
7. Howard Pierce, interview.

Lines

1. Feild, 52.
2. Buten, 139.
3. Buten, 140.
4. Morris, 193.
5. Ellen Pierce, correspondence.
6. Dommel, 13.
7. Larousse Encyclopedia of Animal Life, 612.
8. Striner, 6.
9. Picciotto, correspondence.
10. Ibid.

Porcelain Products

1. Picciotto, interview.
2. Tarrant, 3.
3. Taylor, 10.
4. Taylor, 6.
5. Lynnlee, 5.
6. Ibid.
7. Christenson, 33.
8. Schaut, 4.
9. Shedd, 6.
10. Cushion, 9.

11. Nature in America, 290.
12. "contemporary porcelain: howard pierce design." N. S. Gustin Company marketing brochure.
13. Ellen Pierce, interview.
14. "contemporary porcelain: howard pierce design." N. S. Gustin Company marketing brochure.
15. Ibid.

Other Media

1. Doulton, 44.
2. Jerry Pierce, correspondence.
3. Picciotto, interview.

Outdoor Sculptures

1. Ross, 12.
2. Riley, B3.
3. Cornett, 143.
4. Riley, B3.

Military

1. Ellen Pierce, interview.
2. Brigadier General H. G. Glasgow, personal letter to Howard and Ellen Pierce, March 26, 1981.
3. Brigadier General M. T. Cooper, personal letter to Mr. and Mrs. Howard Pierce, December 22, 1987.
4. President Ronald Reagan, personal letter to Howard Pierce, August 20, 1985.
5. Marine Corp Air Ground Combat Center Officers' Wives' Club Recognition Certificate, December 10, 1992.
6. Martinez.
7. Jenkins, 7.
8. Ibid.
9. Dommel, "Collect the American Eagle," 60.
10. Dommel, 61.
11. Nash.
12. Spangenberg, B2.

Community

1. Mireles, 7.
2. "Statue gets new setting," Hi-Desert Star, November 22, 1989, A3.
3. "Historic kiln donated to Copper Mountain," Hi-Desert Star (February 7, 1992) A8.
4. Helm.
5. "Morongo Basin artist recalled," Hi-Desert Star (March 2, 1994) A10.
6. Janet Pierce Self, interview.
7. Hi-Desert Nature Museum brochure.
8. De Lacy, 46.
9. De Lacy, 48.
10. "Sculptor's donation gives college a weighty welcome," Hi-Desert Star (July 2, 1986).
11. "Statue gets new setting," A3.
12. "Sculptor's donation gives college a weighty welcome."
13. "Statue gets new setting," A3.

Conculsion

1. Mireles, 7.
2. Nelson, 15.
3. Dornhauser, 9.
4. Evans, 6.
5. McGuire, Introduction.
6. Keen, 129.
7. Schneider, 22.

BIBLIOGRAPHY

"And now, a 400-pound roadrunner," *The Daily Enterprise*, June 21, 1972, page C-2.

Andersen, Timothy J., Moore, Eudorah M. and Winter, Robert W., Editors. *California Design 1910*. Salt Lake City, Utah: Peregrine Smith Books, 1974.

Binns, Charles F. "Clay in the Potter's Hand," *The Craftsman*, paper on file at the Elwyn B. Robinson Department of Special Collections, Chester Fritz Library, University of North Dakota, Grand Forks, North Dakota, pages 162-168.

———.*The Potter's Craft*. Princeton, New Jersey: D. Van Norstrand Company, Inc., 1910.

Blietz, Diane. "Basin sculptor closes ceramic studio for good," *Hi-Desert Star*, pages A1 and 2.

Bray, Hazel V. *The Potter's Art in California 1885 to 1955*. Oakland, California: The Oak land Museum Art Department, 1980.

Buten, David. *Eighteenth Century Wedgwood: A Guide for Collectors and Connoisseurs*. New York: Methuen, Inc., 1980.

Casson, Michael. *The Craft of the Potter*. Woodbury, New York: Barron's Educational Series, Inc., 1977.

Chipman, Jack. *Collector's Encyclopedia of California Pottery*. Paducah, Kentucky: Collector Books, 1992.

Christenson, David, "Club convenes to compare cat collections," *The Old Times,* January, 1997, pages 1, 33 and 36.

Cockrum, E. Lendell. *Mammals of the Southwest.* Tucson, Arizona: The University of Arizona Press, 1982.

"contemporary porcelain: howard pierce design." N. S. Gustin Company marketing brochure.

Cooper, M. T., Brigadier General, personal letter to Mr. and Mrs. Howard Pierce, December 22, 1987.

Cornett, James W. *Wildlife of the North American Desert*. Palm Springs, California: Nature Trails Press, 1987.

Cornfield, Betty and Owen Edwards. *Quintessence: The Quality of Having It*. New York: Crown Publishers Inc., 1983.

Cox, Susan N., "Howard Pierce Porcelains," *The Antique Trader Annual of Articles Volume XVI*, pages 14 – 17.

———.Editor, *Twentieth Century American Ceramics Price Guide*. Dubuque, Iowa: Antique Trader Brooks, 1996.

Cushion, John P. *Animals in Pottery and Porcelain*. New York: Crown Publishers, Inc., 1974.

De Lacy, Bob. "Great Horned Owl," *Hi-Desert Magazine,* Spring, 1992, pages 46–48.

Derwich, Jenny B. and Dr. Mary Latos. *Dictionary Guide to United States Pottery and Porcelain*. Franklin, Michigan: Jenstan, 1984.

Dommel, Darlene Hurst. "Collect the American Eagle," *The Antique Trader*, September 29, 1976, pages 60 and 61.

———. *Collector's Encyclopedia of the Dakota Potteries*. Paducah, Kentucky: Collector Books, 1996.

Dornhauser, Paul S. *History of American Ceramics*: The Studio Potter. Dubuque, Iowa: Kendall/Hunt Publishing Company, 1978.

Doulton, Michael. *Discovering Royal Doulton*. Shrewsbury, England: Swan Hill Press, 1993.

Earle, W. Hubert. *Cacti Wildflowers and Desert Plants of Arizona*. Phoenix, Arizona: Desert Botanical Garden of Arizona, 1971.

Evans, Paul. *Art Pottery of the United States*. New York: Feingold and Lewis Publishing Corporation, 1987.

Feild, Rachael. *Buying Antique Pottery and Porcelain*. Radnor, Pennsylvania: Wallace-Homestead Book Company, 1987.

Galloway, Eileen. "Howard Pierce remembered," *Hi-Desert Nature Museum Association Bulletin,* March 1994.

Garfield, Viola E. *Meet the Totem*. Sitka, Alaska, 1961.

Glasgow, H. G., Brigadier General, personal letter to Howard and Ellen Pierce, March 26, 1981.

Graber, Kay, Editor. *Sister to the Sioux: The Memoirs of Elaine Goodale Eastman*. Lincoln, Nebraska: Univeristy of Nebraska Press, 1978.

Helm, Pat. "Myrtle the Turtle Dons New Shell," *The Sun-Telegram*, February 14, 1971.

Herr, Jeffrey. *California Art Pottery 1895-1920: A Catalogue for the Exhibition at California State University Northridge October 31–December 2, 1988*. Northridge, California: California State University, 1988.

Hi-Desert Nature Museum brochure.

"Historic kiln donated to Copper Mountain," *Hi-Desert Star*, February 7, 1992, page A8.

Holmes, Marjorie. *Beauty in Your Own Backyard*. McLean, Virginia: EPM Publications, Inc., 1978.
Hughes, G. Bernard. *The Antique Collector's Pocket Book*. New York: Hawthorn Books, Inc., 1965.
Husfloen, Kyle, Editor. *Pottery and Porcelain Ceramics Price Guide.* Dubuque, Iowa: Antique Trader Books, 1994.
Jenkins, Scott SSGT. "Sentinel stands guard over general's parade field." *Observation Post*, May 13, 1994, pages 6 and 7.
Johnson, Gaylord. *Nature's Program*. Garden City, New York: Nelson Doubleday, Inc., 1926.
Keen, Sam. *Hymns to an Unknown God: Awakening the Spirit in Everyday Life*. New York: Bantam Books, 1994.
Larousse Encyclopedia of Animal Life. New York: The Hamlyn Publishing Group Limited, 1967.
Lehner, Lois. *Lehner's Encyclopedia of U. S. Marks on Pottery, Porcelain and Clay.* Paducah, Kentucky: Collector Books, 1988.
Lewis, David. *Warren MacKenzie, Potter: A Retrospective.* Minneapolis, Minnesota: University Art Museum, 1989.
Lubbock, Sir John. *The Peasures of Life*. Chicago: M. A. Donohue and Company, 1887.
Lynnlee, J. L. *Purrrfection: The Cat*. West Chester, Pennsylvania: Schiffer Publishing Ltd., 1990.
Marine Corp Air Ground Combat Center Officers' Wives' Club Recognition Certificate, December 10, 1992.
Martinez, Anthony Lance CPL. "JT artist donates 12-foot eagle to the combat center," *Observation Post*, June 12, 1985.
McGuire, William. *From Tolkien to Oz*. Parsippany, New Jersey: The Unicorn Publishing House, 1985.
Mireles, Sonia Aguilar. "Looking at life through the eyes of Howard Pierce, extraordinary artist of the Hi-Desert," *Hi-Desert Star Sunday Magazine*, January 15, 1989, pages 6–8.
Mobil Travel Guide: California and the West. New York: Prentice Hall, 1990.
"Morongo Basin artist recalled," *Hi-Desert Star*, March 2, 1994, page A10.
Morris, William, Editor. *The American Heritage Dictionary*. Boston: Houghton Mifflin Company, 1976.
Nash, Christopher. "Post Mascot: Symbol of Care and Concern," *Monitor*, March 27, 1989.
Nature in America. Pleasantville, New York: The Reader's Digest Association, Inc., 1991.
Nelson, Marion John. *Art Pottery of the Midwest*. Minneapolis, Minnesota: University Art Museum, 1988.
Off the Beaten Path. Pleasantville, New York: The Reader's Digest Association, Inc. 1987.
Olin, George. *Animals of the Southwest Deserts.* Gila Pueblo, Globe, Arizona: Southwestern Monuments Association, 1954.
Olson, Sigurd E. *Reflections from the North County*. New York: Alfred A Knopf, 1978.
Pellecchia, Michael. "Engelbreit's lessons on using talent go beyond art," *Star Tribune*, November 22, 1996, page E11.
Picciotto, Linda Pierce. "HW Pierce Glazes and Clay: Notes From My Notebook," 1996.
———.British Columbia, Canada, in person interviews March 1996, correspondence and telephone interviews.
Pierce, Ellen, California, in-person interviews November 1991, March 1992, April 1995, August 1995 and March 1996, correspondence and telephone interviews.
Pierce, Howard, Joshua Tree, California, in person interviews November 1991 and March 1992, and telephone interviews.
Pierce, Jerry, California, in-person interviews August 1995, and correspondence.
President Ronald Reagan, personal letter to Howard Pierce, August 20, 1985.
"Puffed Tuffins." *International Wildlife*, July–August, 1989, page 12.
"Remembering Friends," *Friends of CMC Reporter*, Spring 1994.
Richey, Tina A. "Collectors are discovering Brayton Laguna Pottery," *Antique Week*, March 11, 1996, pages 2 and 30.
Riley, Joan. "Artist ideas are cast in cement," *The Coloradon*, Fort Collins, Colorado, October 15, 1981.
Giant animal sculptures on art tour," *The Sun*, October 3, 1981, page B3.
"Robinsons' Gift Accents 1941," *Vogue*, 1941.
Ross, Marty. "Gardens alive!" *Star Tribune Home and Garden,* August 29, 1996, page 12.
Schaut, Jim and Nancy. *"Horsin' Around": A Price Guide on Horse Collectibles*. Gas City, Indiana: L-W Book Sales, 1990.
Schneider, Mike. *Animal Figures*. West Chester, Pennsylvania: Schiffer Publishing Ltd., 1990.

———. *California Potteries*. Atglen, Pennsylvania: Schiffer Publishing Ltd., 1995.
"Sculptor's donation gives college a weighty welcome," *Hi-Desert Star*, July 2, 1986.
Self, Janet Pierce, California, in-person interviews March 1996, correspondence and telephone interviews.
Shedd, Warner. *The Kids' Wildlife Book*. Charlotte, Vermont: Williamson Publishing, 1994.
Spangenberg, Margot. "Pierce exhibit at museum," August 29, 1996, page B2.
"Statue gets new setting," *Hi-Desert Star,* November 22, 1989, page A3.
Striner, Richard. *Art Deco*. New York: Abbeville Press, 1994.
Tarrant, Bill. *The Magic of Dogs*. New York: Lyons-Burford, 1995.
Taylor, David. *The Ultimate Dog Book*. New York: Simon and Schuster, 1990.
"The British Virgin Islands," promotional brochure, New York: British Virgin Islands Tourist Board, 1994.
Trapp, Kenneth R. *The Arts and Crafts Movement in California: Living the Good Life*. New York: Abbeville Press, 1993.
"Two men will be missed," Hi-Desert Star, March 6, 1994, page A4.
Welles, Phillip. *Meet the Southwest Deserts.* Tucson, Arizona: Dale Stuart King, 1964.
Wissinger, Joanna. *Arts and Crafts Pottery and Ceramics.* San Francisco: Chronicle Books, 1994.
Zim, Herbert S. and Donald F. Hoffmeister *Mammals*. New York: Golden Press, 1987.

ABOUT THE AUTHOR

Darlene Hurst Dommel was initally attracted to the distinctive style of Howard Pierce porcelains, discovering quality and uniqueness. As Howard Pierce captured the essence of animals and birds in his figures, the writer has attempted in this book to capture the essence of this outstanding artist.

Darlene, who holds a research-oriented master of science degree, has had over 25 years experience researching and writing about American art pottery. She has had over 50 magazine articles published in the antiques field and is the author of the lauded *Collector's Encyclopedia of the Dakota Potteries* published in 1996.

INDEX

COLLECTOR BOOKS

Informing Today's Collector

For over two decades we have been keeping collectors informed on trends and values in all fields of antiques and collectibles.

DOLLS, FIGURES & TEDDY BEARS

4707 A Decade of **Barbie** Dolls & Collectibles, 1981–1991, Summers $19.95
4631 **Barbie** Doll Boom, 1986–1995, Augustyniak $18.95
2079 **Barbie** Doll Fashions, Volume I, Eames $24.95
3957 **Barbie** Exclusives, Rana $18.95
4632 **Barbie** Exclusives, Book II, Rana $18.95
4557 **Barbie,** The First 30 Years, Deutsch $24.95
4657 **Barbie** Years, 1959–1995, Olds $16.95
3310 **Black Dolls,** 1820–1991, Perkins $17.95
3873 **Black Dolls,** Book II, Perkins $17.95
1529 Collector's Encyclopedia of **Barbie** Dolls, DeWein $19.95
4506 Collector's Guide to **Dolls in Uniform,** Bourgeois $18.95
3727 Collector's Guide to **Ideal Dolls,** Izen $18.95
3728 Collector's Guide to Miniature **Teddy Bears,** Powell $17.95
3967 Collector's Guide to **Trolls,** Peterson $19.95
4571 **Liddle Kiddles,** Identification & Value Guide, Langford $18.95
4645 **Madame Alexander** Dolls Price Guide #21, Smith $9.95
3733 **Modern Collector's** Dolls, Sixth Series, Smith $24.95
3991 **Modern Collector's** Dolls, Seventh Series, Smith $24.95
4647 **Modern Collector's** Dolls, Eighth Series, Smith $24.95
4640 Patricia Smith's **Doll Values,** Antique to Modern, 12th Edition $12.95
3826 Story of **Barbie,** Westenhouser $19.95
1513 **Teddy Bears & Steiff** Animals, Mandel $9.95
1817 **Teddy Bears & Steiff** Animals, 2nd Series, Mandel $19.95
2084 **Teddy Bears, Annalee's & Steiff** Animals, 3rd Series, Mandel $19.95
1808 Wonder of **Barbie,** Manos $9.95
1430 World of **Barbie** Dolls, Manos $9.95

FURNITURE

1457 American **Oak** Furniture, McNerney $9.95
3716 American **Oak** Furniture, Book II, McNerney $12.95
1118 Antique **Oak** Furniture, Hill $7.95
2132 Collector's Encyclopedia of **American** Furniture, Vol. I, Swedberg $24.95
2271 Collector's Encyclopedia of **American** Furniture, Vol. II, Swedberg $24.95
3720 Collector's Encyclopedia of **American** Furniture, Vol. III, Swedberg $24.95
3878 Collector's Guide to **Oak** Furniture, George $12.95
1755 Furniture of the **Depression Era,** Swedberg $19.95
3906 **Heywood-Wakefield** Modern Furniture, Rouland $18.95
1885 **Victorian** Furniture, Our American Heritage, McNerney $9.95
3829 **Victorian** Furniture, Our American Heritage, Book II, McNerney $9.95
3869 **Victorian** Furniture books, 2 volume set, McNerney $19.90

JEWELRY, HATPINS, WATCHES & PURSES

1712 Antique & Collector's **Thimbles** & Accessories, Mathis $19.95
1748 Antique **Purses,** Revised Second Ed., Holiner $19.95
1278 Art Nouveau & Art Deco **Jewelry,** Baker $9.95
4558 **Christmas Pins,** Past and Present, Gallina $18.95
3875 Collecting Antique **Stickpins,** Kerins $16.95
3722 Collector's Ency. of **Compacts, Carryalls & Face Powder Boxes,** Mueller ...$24.95
4655 Complete Price Guide to **Watches,** #16, Shugart $26.95
1716 Fifty Years of Collectible **Fashion Jewelry,** 1925-1975, Baker $19.95
1424 **Hatpins** & Hatpin Holders, Baker $9.95
4570 Ladies' **Compacts,** Gerson $24.95
1181 100 Years of Collectible **Jewelry,** 1850-1950, Baker $9.95
2348 20th Century Fashionable Plastic **Jewelry,** Baker $19.95
3830 Vintage **Vanity Bags & Purses,** Gerson $24.95

TOYS, MARBLES & CHRISTMAS COLLECTIBLES

3427 **Advertising Character** Collectibles, Dotz $17.95
2333 Antique & Collector's **Marbles,** 3rd Ed., Grist $9.95
3827 Antique & Collector's **Toys,** 1870–1950, Longest $24.95
3956 Baby Boomer **Games,** Identification & Value Guide, Polizzi $24.95
3717 **Christmas** Collectibles, 2nd Edition, Whitmyer $24.95
1752 **Christmas** Ornaments, Lights & Decorations, Johnson $19.95
4649 Classic Plastic **Model Kits,** Polizzi $24.95
4559 Collectible **Action Figures,** 2nd Ed., Manos $17.95
3874 Collectible Coca-Cola Toy **Trucks,** deCourtivron $24.95
2338 Collector's Encyclopedia of **Disneyana,** Longest, Stern $24.95
4639 Collector's Guide to **Diecast Toys & Scale Models,** Johnson $19.95
4651 Collector's Guide to **Tinker Toys,** Strange $18.95
4566 Collector's Guide to **Tootsietoys,** 2nd Ed., Richter $19.95
3436 Grist's Big Book of **Marbles** $19.95
3970 Grist's Machine-Made & Contemporary **Marbles,** 2nd Ed. $9.95
4569 **Howdy Doody,** Collector's Reference and Trivia Guide, Koch $16.95
4723 **Matchbox®** Toys, 1948 to 1993, Johnson, 2nd Ed. $18.95
3823 **Mego** Toys, An Illustrated Value Guide, Chrouch 15.95
1540 **Modern Toys** 1930–1980, Baker $19.95
3888 **Motorcycle** Toys, Antique & Contemporary, Gentry/Downs $18.95
4728 Schroeder's Collectible **Toys,** Antique to Modern Price Guide, 3rd Ed. $17.95
1886 Stern's Guide to **Disney** Collectibles $14.95
2139 Stern's Guide to **Disney** Collectibles, 2nd Series $14.95
3975 Stern's Guide to **Disney** Collectibles, 3rd Series $18.95
2028 **Toys,** Antique & Collectible, Longest $14.95
3979 **Zany Characters** of the Ad World, Lamphier $16.95

INDIANS, GUNS, KNIVES, TOOLS, PRIMITIVES

1868 Antique **Tools,** Our American Heritage, McNerney $9.95
2015 Archaic **Indian** Points & Knives, Edler $14.95
1426 **Arrowheads** & Projectile Points, Hothem $7.95
4633 **Big Little Books,** Jacobs $18.95
2279 **Indian** Artifacts of the Midwest, Hothem $14.95
3885 **Indian** Artifacts of the Midwest, Book II, Hothem $16.95
1964 **Indian** Axes & Related Stone Artifacts, Hothem $14.95
2023 **Keen Kutter** Collectibles, Heuring $14.95
4724 Modern **Guns,** Identification & Values, 11th Ed., Quertermous $12.95
4505 Standard Guide to **Razors,** Ritchie & Stewart $9.95
4730 Standard **Knife** Collector's Guide, 3rd Ed., Ritchie & Stewart $12.95

PAPER COLLECTIBLES & BOOKS

4633 **Big Little Books,** Jacobs $18.95
1441 Collector's Guide to **Post Cards,** Wood $9.95
2081 Guide to Collecting **Cookbooks,** Allen $14.95
4648 Huxford's **Old Book** Value Guide, 8th Ed. $19.95
2080 Price Guide to **Cookbooks & Recipe Leaflets,** Dickinson $9.95
2346 **Sheet Music** Reference & Price Guide, 2nd Ed., Pafik & Guiheen $18.95
4654 **Victorian Trading Cards,** Historical Reference & Value Guide, Cheadle $19.95

GLASSWARE

1006 **Cambridge Glass** Reprint 1930–1934 ....$14.95
1007 **Cambridge Glass** Reprint 1949–1953 ....$14.95
4561 Collectible **Drinking Glasses,** Chase & Kelly $17.95
4642 Collectible **Glass Shoes,** Wheatley $19.95
4553 Coll. **Glassware from the 40's, 50's & 60's,** 3rd Ed., Florence $19.95
2352 Collector's Encyclopedia of **Akro Agate Glassware,** Florence $14.95
1810 Collector's Encyclopedia of **American Art Glass,** Shuman $29.95
3312 Collector's Encyclopedia of **Children's Dishes,** Whitmyer $19.95
4552 Collector's Encyclopedia of **Depression Glass,** 12th Ed., Florence $19.95
1664 Collector's Encyclopedia of **Heisey Glass,** 1925–1938, Bredehoft $24.95
3905 Collector's Encyclopedia of **Milk Glass,** Newbound $24.95
1523 Colors In **Cambridge Glass,** National Cambridge Society $19.95
4564 **Crackle Glass,** Weitman $19.95
2275 **Czechoslovakian Glass** and Collectibles, Barta/Rose $16.95
4714 **Czechoslovakian Glass** and Collectibles, Book II, Barta/Rose $16.95
4716 **Elegant Glassware** of the Depression Era, 7th Ed., Florence $19.95
1380 Encylopedia of **Pattern Glass,** McClain $12.95
3981 Ever's Standard **Cut Glass** Value Guide $12.95
4659 **Fenton** Art Glass, 1907–1939, Whitmyer $24.95
3725 **Fostoria,** Pressed, Blown & Hand Molded Shapes, Kerr $24.95
3883 **Fostoria Stemware,** The Crystal for America, Long & Seate $24.95
3318 **Glass Animals** of the Depression Era, Garmon & Spencer $19.95
4644 **Imperial Carnival Glass,** Burns $18.95

COLLECTOR BOOKS

Informing Today's Collector

3886 **Kitchen Glassware** of the Depression Years, 5th Ed., Florence $19.95
2394 **Oil Lamps II,** Glass Kerosene Lamps, Thuro $24.95
4725 Pocket Guide to **Depression Glass,** 10th Ed., Florence $9.95
4634 Standard Encylopedia of **Carnival Glass,** 5th Ed., Edwards $24.95
4635 Standard **Carnival Glass** Price Guide, 10th Ed. $9.95
3974 Standard Encylopedia of **Opalescent Glass,** Edwards $19.95
4731 **Stemware Identification,** Featuring Cordials with Values, Florence $24.95
3326 **Very Rare Glassware** of the Depression Years, 3rd Series, Florence $24.95
3909 **Very Rare Glassware** of the Depression Years, 4th Series, Florence $24.95
4732 **Very Rare Glassware** of the Depression Years, 5th Series, Florence $24.95
4656 **Westmoreland Glass,** Wilson $24.95
2224 World of **Salt Shakers,** 2nd Ed., Lechner $24.95

POTTERY

4630 **American Limoges,** Limoges $24.95
1312 **Blue & White Stoneware,** McNerney $9.95
1958 So. Potteries **Blue Ridge Dinnerware,** 3rd Ed., Newbound $14.95
1959 **Blue Willow,** 2nd Ed., Gaston $14.95
3816 Collectible **Vernon Kilns,** Nelson $24.95
3311 Collecting **Yellow Ware** – Id. & Value Guide, McAllister $16.95
1373 Collector's Encyclopedia of **American Dinnerware,** Cunningham $24.95
3815 Collector's Encyclopedia of **Blue Ridge Dinnerware,** Newbound $19.95
4658 Collector's Encyclopedia of **Brush-McCoy Pottery,** Huxford $24.95
2272 Collector's Encyclopedia of **California Pottery,** Chipman $24.95
3811 Collector's Encyclopedia of **Colorado Pottery,** Carlton $24.95
2133 Collector's Encyclopedia of **Cookie Jars,** Roerig $24.95
3723 Collector's Encyclopedia of **Cookie Jars,** Volume II, Roerig $24.95
3429 Collector's Encyclopedia of **Cowan Pottery,** Saloff $24.95
4638 Collector's Encyclopedia of **Dakota Potteries,** Dommel $24.95
2209 Collector's Encyclopedia of **Fiesta,** 7th Ed., Huxford $19.95
4718 Collector's Encyclopedia of **Figural Planters & Vases,** Newbound $19.95
3961 Collector's Encyclopedia of **Early Noritake,** Alden $24.95
1439 Collector's Encyclopedia of **Flow Blue China,** Gaston $19.95
3812 Collector's Encyclopedia of **Flow Blue China,** 2nd Ed., Gaston $24.95
3813 Collector's Encyclopedia of **Hall China,** 2nd Ed., Whitmyer $24.95
3431 Collector's Encyclopedia of **Homer Laughlin China,** Jasper $24.95
1276 Collector's Encyclopedia of **Hull Pottery,** Roberts $19.95
4573 Collector's Encyclopedia of **Knowles, Taylor & Knowles,** Gaston $24.95
3962 Collector's Encyclopedia of **Lefton China,** DeLozier $19.95
2210 Collector's Encyclopedia of **Limoges Porcelain,** 2nd Ed., Gaston $24.95
2334 Collector's Encyclopedia of **Majolica Pottery,** Katz-Marks $19.95
1358 Collector's Encyclopedia of **McCoy Pottery,** Huxford $19.95
3963 Collector's Encyclopedia of **Metlox Potteries,** Gibbs Jr. $24.95
3313 Collector's Encyclopedia of **Niloak,** Gifford $19.95
3837 Collector's Encyclopedia of **Nippon Porcelain I,** Van Patten $24.95
2089 Collector's Ency. of **Nippon Porcelain,** 2nd Series, Van Patten $24.95
1665 Collector's Ency. of **Nippon Porcelain,** 3rd Series, Van Patten $24.95
3836 **Nippon Porcelain** Price Guide, Van Patten $9.95
1447 Collector's Encyclopedia of **Noritake,** Van Patten $19.95
3432 Collector's Encyclopedia of **Noritake,** 2nd Series, Van Patten $24.95
1037 Collector's Encyclopedia of **Occupied Japan,** Vol. I, Florence $14.95
1038 Collector's Encyclopedia of **Occupied Japan,** Vol. II, Florence $14.95
2088 Collector's Encyclopedia of **Occupied Japan,** Vol. III, Florence $14.95
2019 Collector's Encyclopedia of **Occupied Japan,** Vol. IV, Florence $14.95
2335 Collector's Encyclopedia of **Occupied Japan,** Vol. V, Florence $14.95
3964 Collector's Encyclopedia of **Pickard China,** Reed $24.95
1311 Collector's Encyclopedia of **R.S. Prussia,** 1st Series, Gaston $24.95
1715 Collector's Encyclopedia of **R.S. Prussia,** 2nd Series, Gaston $24.95
3726 Collector's Encyclopedia of **R.S. Prussia,** 3rd Series, Gaston $24.95
3877 Collector's Encyclopedia of **R.S. Prussia,** 4th Series, Gaston $24.95
1034 Collector's Encyclopedia of **Roseville Pottery,** Huxford $19.95
1035 Collector's Encyclopedia of **Roseville Pottery,** 2nd Ed., Huxford $19.95
3357 **Roseville** Price Guide No. 10 ....$9.95
3965 Collector's Encyclopedia of **Sascha Brastoff,** Conti, Bethany & Seay $24.95
3314 Collector's Encyclopedia of **Van Briggle** Art Pottery, Sasicki $24.95
4563 Collector's Encyclopedia of **Wall Pockets,** Newbound $19.95
2111 Collector's Encyclopedia of **Weller Pottery,** Huxford $29.95
3452 Coll. Guide to **Country Stoneware & Pottery,** Raycraft $11.95
2077 Coll. Guide to **Country Stoneware & Pottery,** 2nd Series, Raycraft $14.95
3434 Coll. Guide to **Hull Pottery,** The Dinnerware Line, Gick-Burke $16.95
3876 Collector's Guide to **Lu-Ray Pastels,** Meehan $18.95
3814 Collector's Guide to **Made in Japan** Ceramics, White $18.95
4646 Collector's Guide to **Made in Japan** Ceramics, Book II, White $18.95
4565 Collector's Guide to **Rockingham,** The Enduring Ware, Brewer $14.95
2339 Collector's Guide to **Shawnee Pottery,** Vanderbilt $19.95
1425 **Cookie Jars,** Westfall $9.95
3440 **Cookie Jars,** Book II, Westfall $19.95
3435 Debolt's Dictionary of **American Pottery Marks** $17.95
2379 Lehner's Ency. of **U.S. Marks** on Pottery, Porcelain & China $24.95
4722 **McCoy Pottery,** Collector's Reference & Value Guide, Hanson/Nissen $19.95
3825 **Puritan Pottery,** Morris $24.95
4726 **Red Wing Art Pottery,** 1920s–1960s, Dollen $19.95
1670 **Red Wing Collectibles,** DePasquale $9.95
1440 **Red Wing Stoneware,** DePasquale $9.95
3738 **Shawnee Pottery,** Mangus $24.95
4629 Turn of the Century **American Dinnerware,** 1880s–1920s, Jasper $24.95
4572 **Wall Pockets** of the Past, Perkins $17.95
3327 **Watt Pottery** – Identification & Value Guide, Morris $19.95

OTHER COLLECTIBLES

4704 Antique & Collectible **Buttons,** Wisniewski $19.95
2269 Antique **Brass & Copper** Collectibles, Gaston $16.95
1880 Antique **Iron,** McNerney $9.95
3872 Antique **Tins,** Dodge $24.95
1714 **Black** Collectibles, Gibbs $19.95
1128 **Bottle** Pricing Guide, 3rd Ed., Cleveland $7.95
4636 **Celluloid Collectibles,** Dunn $14.95
3959 **Cereal Box** Bonanza, The 1950's, Bruce $19.95
3718 Collectible **Aluminum,** Grist $16.95
3445 Collectible **Cats,** An Identification & Value Guide, Fyke $18.95
4560 Collectible **Cats,** An Identification & Value Guide, Book II, Fyke $19.95
1634 Collector's Ency. of Figural & Novelty **Salt & Pepper Shakers,** Davern $19.95
2020 Collector's Ency. of Figural & Novelty **Salt & Pepper Shakers,** Vol. II, Davern ..$19.95
2018 Collector's Encyclopedia of **Granite Ware,** Greguire $24.95
3430 Collector's Encyclopedia of **Granite Ware,** Book II, Greguire $24.95
4705 Collector's Guide to **Antique Radios,** 4th Ed., Bunis $18.95
1916 Collector's Guide to **Art Deco,** Gaston $14.95
3880 Collector's Guide to **Cigarette Lighters,** Flanagan $17.95
4637 Collector's Guide to **Cigarette Lighters,** Book II, Flanagan $17.95
1537 Collector's Guide to **Country Baskets,** Raycraft $9.95
3966 Collector's Guide to **Inkwells,** Identification & Values, Badders $18.95
3881 Collector's Guide to **Novelty Radios,** Bunis/Breed $18.95
4652 Collector's Guide to **Transistor Radios,** 2nd Ed., Bunis $16.95
4653 Collector's Guide to **TV Memorabilia,** 1960s–1970s, Davis/Morgan $24.95
2276 **Decoys,** Kangas $24.95
1629 **Doorstops,** Identification & Values, Bertoia $9.95
4567 Figural **Napkin Rings,** Gottschalk & Whitson $18.95
3968 **Fishing Lure** Collectibles, Murphy/Edmisten $24.95
3817 **Flea Market Trader,** 10th Ed., Huxford $12.95
3976 Foremost Guide to **Uncle Sam** Collectibles, Czulewicz $24.95
4641 **Garage Sale & Flea Market Annual,** 4th Ed. $19.95
3819 **General Store Collectibles,** Wilson $24.95
4643 **Great American West** Collectibles, Wilson $24.95
2215 Goldstein's **Coca-Cola** Collectibles $16.95
3884 Huxford's Collectible **Advertising,** 2nd Ed. $24.95
2216 **Kitchen Antiques,** 1790–1940, McNerney $14.95
3321 Ornamental & Figural **Nutcrackers,** Rittenhouse $16.95
2026 **Railroad** Collectibles, 4th Ed., Baker $14.95
1632 **Salt & Pepper Shakers,** Guarnaccia $9.95
1888 **Salt & Pepper Shakers** II, Identification & Value Guide, Book II, Guarnaccia ..$14.95
2220 **Salt & Pepper Shakers** III, Guarnaccia $14.95
3443 **Salt & Pepper Shakers** IV, Guarnaccia $18.95
4555 **Schroeder's Antiques Price Guide,** 14th Ed., Huxford $12.95
2096 **Silverplated Flatware,** Revised 4th Edition, Hagan $14.95
1922 Standard **Old Bottle** Price Guide, Sellari $14.95
4708 Summers' Guide to **Coca-Cola** $19.95
3892 **Toy & Miniature Sewing Machines,** Thomas $18.95
3828 Value Guide to **Advertising Memorabilia,** Summers $18.95
3977 Value Guide to **Gas Station** Memorabilia, Summers & Priddy $24.95
3444 **Wanted to Buy,** 5th Edition $9.95

This is only a partial listing of the books on antiques that are available from Collector Books. All books are well illustrated and contain current values. Most of these books are available from your local bookseller, antique dealer, or public library. If you are unable to locate certain titles in your area, you may order by mail from COLLECTOR BOOKS, P.O. Box 3009, Paducah, KY 42002-3009. Customers with Visa or MasterCard may phone in orders from 7:00–5:00 CST, Monday–Friday, Toll Free 1-800-626-5420. Add $2.00 for postage for the first book ordered and $0.30 for each additional book. Include item number, title, and price when ordering. Allow 14 to 21 days for delivery.

Schroeder's ANTIQUES Price Guide

. . . is the #1 best-selling antiques & collectibles value guide on the market today, and here's why . . .

8½ x 11, 608 Pages, $12.95

- *More than 300 advisors, well-known dealers, and top-notch collectors work together with our editors to bring you accurate information regarding pricing and identification.*

- *More than 45,000 items in almost 500 categories are listed along with hundreds of sharp original photos that illustrate not only the rare and unusual, but the common, popular collectibles as well.*

- *Each large close-up shot shows important details clearly. Every subject is represented with histories and background information, a feature not found in any of our competitors' publications.*

- *Our editors keep abreast of newly developing trends, often adding several new categories a year as the need arises.*

If it merits the interest of today's collector, you'll find it in *Schroeder's*. And you can feel confident that the information we publish is up to date and accurate. Our advisors thoroughly check each category to spot inconsistencies, listings that may not be entirely reflective of market dealings, and lines too vague to be of merit. Only the best of the lot remains for publication.

Without doubt, you'll find
SCHROEDER'S ANTIQUES PRICE GUIDE
the only one to buy for
reliable information and values.

COLLECTOR BOOKS

A Division of Schroeder Publishing Co., Inc.